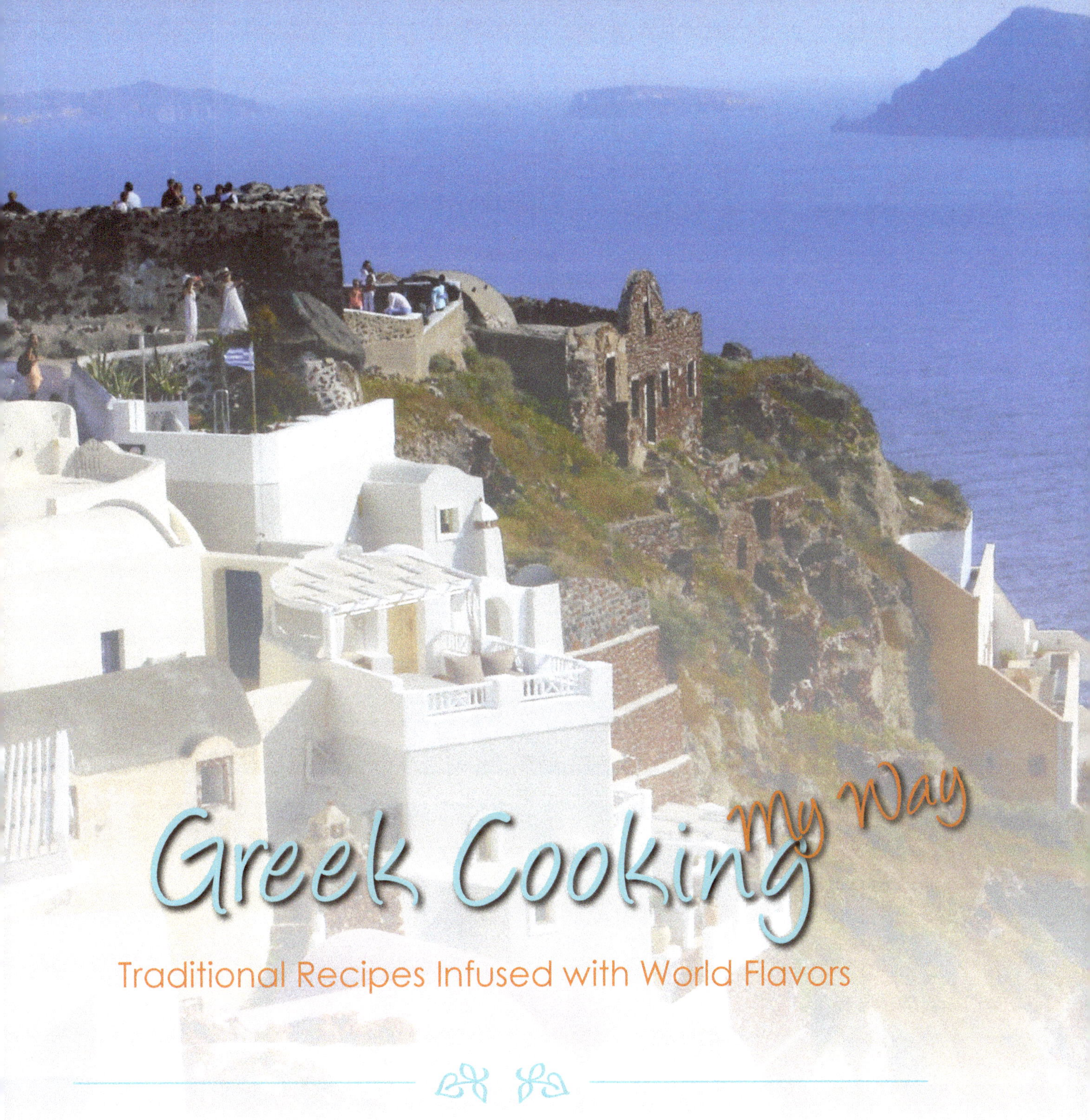

Greek Cooking My Way

Traditional Recipes Infused with World Flavors

Chef Stefania

Greek Cooking My Way by Stefania Luxenberg

Publisher: Chef Stef Publishing

For information including purchasing books, visit our website at: https://chefsteflux.com.

Have Spatula – Will Travel

Editor: John Luxenberg
Creative Consultant: John Luxenberg
ISBN-13: 978-0-9995949-0-2
First Edition
Printed and bound in United States of America

Table of Contents

Dedication

This book is dedicated to my husband, John,
for his love, encouragement and constant support.

Acknowledgements

Louise and Len	Motivation, Inspiration, Encouragement
John Luxenberg	Producer, Writer, Photographer
Jordan Best	Graphic Designer
Avery Caldwell	Graphic Designer
Kathryn and Shelton Green	Proofreaders, Photo Equipment
Gilberto Cardenas	Photographer
Irini Cardenas	Food Stylist
Angeli Menta	Proofreader
Tiffany Kessler	Proofreader
My daughter, Anna	Photographs
My granddaughter, Maya	Photographs
My grandson, Mikkel	Photographs
Angeliki Kassalia	Photographs
Vivia Costales	Support
My son, Alexandros	Support
My sisters, Eirini and Mary	Support
My friends	Support

Preface

I was born on a small Greek island, Syros, where cooking was always an integral part of my family. It brought the family together over the dining table where we talked and laughed while discussing our lives.

It was on this small island that I learned the art of cooking from my grandmother, aunt, and mother who inspired me to love preparing food. I remember my grandmother cooking on a wood-burning stove; I was constantly interested in what she was creating. She ingrained in me her cooking philosophy, often mentioning to caress and treat my food as if it were my lover.

My mother and aunt concocted delectable preserves from rose leaves and lemon flowers whose heavenly scents permeated our home. Thus began my culinary odyssey of preparing tasty cuisine while teaching others – including my children – about the pleasures of the wonderful world of food. Soon friends looked forward to coming to my house to enjoy a hearty meal, fun, and conversation. They would compliment me as they asked me to cook for a wedding, event opening, party, or holiday.

Their encouragement led to the start of my first restaurant, Monopolio, in Syros. It was often crowded with hungry, excited patrons where the dishes were custom-created "My Way." Customers commented, "You taught us how to eat" (see page 163) as the restaurant received high praise in many newspapers and magazines. This paved the way for several appearances on Greek television.

My second Greek restaurant, Fox, also located in Syros, received many positive reviews. This gave me the opportunity to be an integral member of the Greek Culinary Presentation Team at the Culinary Institute of America's 12th Annual Flavors of the World International Conference and Festival in Napa Valley, California. Later, I was invited to the United States to prepare cuisine for a successful entrepreneur. While in the United States I had the very good fortune of meeting my husband, and to work for more entrepreneurs who liked my family's recipes and encouraged me to write this cookbook. And so, this book is composed of my adaptation of numerous recipes, tips, hints, and suggestions passed down from my family. I hope that when you prepare these recipes, you experience the same wonderful feelings that I did as a child, and now as an adult.

*I hope you enjoy the recipes in "Greek Cooking **My Way**."*

Chapter 1

Herbs Galore and More

No Herb Left Unpicked

Sitting on a beach towel, Demetris, a 35-year-old pharmaceutical salesman, guzzles Mythos beer with his bikini-clad girlfriend, Eleni. She's in her late twenties, beautiful and radiant.

They're enjoying Agathopes beach, which is located on the Greek island of Syros in the Aegean Sea south of Athens. The deep blue sky enhances this fantastic day. Small turquoise waves break at the shoreline. However, as the sun beats down, the temperature soars to over 100 degrees.

The amorous couple gazes at each other, clicks their bottles, and gulps more beer. Soon, they can no longer take the heat. They hastily pack and jump in an old Fiat with Eleni driving to her residence.

Demetris grabs his stomach, and turns to Eleni pleading,

DEMETRIS
(desperately)
Eleni, we better head for the nearest drug store. I got a horrific stomach ache. I need some antacids.

ELENI
Pills, pills, pills. That's always your answer for what ails you.

DEMETRIS
What do ya expect? I'm a pill pusher. That's my job. I suppose you got a better idea?

ELENI
How 'bout trying a natural cure?

DEMETRIS
Natural? Like what? Come on; just find a drug store. Quickly!

ELENI
Is some herbal tea really going to hurt you?

DEMETRIS
Eleni! Just find a pharmacy!

Eleni abruptly pulls the car off the road and slams on the brakes, jerking the car's occupants forward. The newly-created dust cloud envelops the car. Coughing, Eleni jumps from the car and...

DEMETRIS
Eleni, get back in here!

... darts to the side of the road.

ELENI
This is my pharmacy!

It appears there are a variety of weeds growing on the side of the road... But, they're not weeds. They're wild thyme, sage and chamomile, which can enhance a dish's flavor or be used to make a soothing tea.

Eleni quickly picks a variety of natural herbs and jumps back in the car.

DEMETRIS
What the heck you gonna do with those weeds? Honey, I need some pills.

ELENI
I guarantee you'll feel better twenty minutes after we get home.

Eleni pulls her car into the driveway of a vintage Greek villa. Moments later in her simple kitchen, she washes the chamomile and brews a special tea. She pours this over ice, adds a dash of honey as well as several mint leaves, and proudly carries a tray of her iced creation to a groaning Demetris who's sprawled on the living room couch. He reluctantly takes a sip.

DEMETRIS
Hey, this is delicious!

Fifteen minutes later-

DEMETRIS
Baby, I feel great. What was in that tea?

From the kitchen Eleni yells,

ELENI
Just some natural stuff.

DEMETRIS
Please, Honey. Tell me. I need to call my company. They can make it into a pill. I'll get a raise for sure.

Forty-five minutes later Eleni brings a sizzling chicken dinner enhanced with wild sage to the dining room. Demetris gives Eleni an amorous glance as they sip great Greek wine while enjoying a romantic dinner and watching a dazzling Aegean sunset.

Chives
Bay Leaves
Rosemary
Parsley
Thyme
Sage

My Essential Herbs for Greek Cuisine

Herbs in Greece have been used for generations for flavor and medicinal purposes. This was first made apparent to me when my grandmother, Maria, put me on her knee and explained the "Herbs of Life."

This conversation was essential because unique herbs and spices grow so profusely in Greece that you cannot avoid crushing them as you walk. Their fragrances permeate every island. My mother, Kaliope, always had olive oil she enhanced with oregano, thyme, rosemary and a bay leaf as well as vinegar enriched with rose petals to flavor salads and other dishes.

Later, as a Greek chef, I did not have to spend exorbitant amounts of money for a handful of pre-packaged supermarket herbs that were far from fresh. Often when walking or driving through the narrow island roads, I stopped to pick fresh herbs for my cooking. They are an integral part of Greek cuisine. Included below are some of the most important herbs I use in "Greek Cooking My Way."

Basil (*Bassiliko* – which means "king" in Greek)

Basil is one of the great culinary herbs commonly used fresh in cooked recipes. It is best to add this herb at the last moment as cooking quickly destroys its flavor. Tomato dishes, chicken, and vegetables all go well with basil. Plus, dried basil has a weaker flavor than fresh basil.

Hint:

Using a knife to cut basil can bruise and darken the leaves. For salads and pasta sauces where appearance matters, carefully shred the leaves with your fingers. Note that young leaves have the best flavor, while old ones have a coarser, stronger taste.

Bay Leaf (*Daphne*)

Bay leaves are used to add a woodsy taste during cooking and are generally removed from the dish before serving. They complement soups, stews, marinades, sauces such as béarnaise, and spice mixes.

Furthermore, Greek mythology gave this herb its Greek name, Daphne, a beautiful nymph, and daughter of the river god, Peneios. The story proclaimed that Daphne later was transformed by her parents into a bay laurel tree in order to retain her virginity. Consequently, the bay laurel tree is associated with purity.

Hint:

To deter weevils from entering your pantry, add bay leaves to containers of flour and rice. Also, the leaves will enrich the smell of the area.

Capers (*Kapari*)

Capers are a very distinctive ingredient in Greek and Italian cuisine, and are picked in the summer months.

The caper bush grows wild on most of the Greek islands, especially in the Cyclades Islands where plants tumble over inaccessible cliffs often making accessibility very difficult.

Salt-cured capers from a glass jar taste delicious, and are used in many kinds of white and red sauces, on top of fish, and in the traditional Greek salad.

Hint:

If the caper buds are not picked, they create beautiful flowers which open at night. The caper produces a fruit called a caper berry which can be pickled and later served as a Greek appetizer (*mezze*).

Caper leaves, which are hard to find outside of Greece or Cyprus, are used frequently in salads or fish dishes. They're pickled or boiled, and preserved in jars with brine like caper buds.

Mint (*Dyosmos*)

In Greece you can find dried and fresh mint in markets. It's used in everything from cheese dishes to tomato-basil sauce, meatballs, lamb and stuffed vegetable dishes.

Hint:

Mint is also used as a tea. Mint tea is not only good for you, but it's tasty hot or cold. In Greece mint is used as a folk remedy for stomach aches.

Brewing instructions:

Add half a cup of cleaned, rinsed mint leaves to one quart of boiling water. Let the mixture stand a few minutes to brew and cool before drinking.

Oregano (*Rigani*)

Oregano is indigenous to Greece. This important culinary herb can be found in mountainous and rocky areas. After oregano is harvested around the end of summer, the leaves and tight flower buds are dried. It's flavorful, aromatic, and normally sprinkled over meat, fish, salads and sauces.

Hint:
Traditionally oregano has been regarded as an herb for the gut. It relieves flatulence and improves digestion as well. Hippocrates used oregano as an antiseptic.

Rosemary (*Dendrolivano*)
Rosemary is aromatic, and used as flavoring in food such as stuffing, roast lamb, pork, chicken, turkey and fish. It goes particularly well as a topping for roast potatoes.

Hint:
The hard stems can be used for skewers to give additional flavor to your dish while barbecuing.

Sage (*Faskomilo*)
This herb grows wild on hillsides throughout the Mediterranean region. Sage has a strong flavor that is spicy and sharp. Small amounts of sage leaves are often used in cooking meats, vegetables, poultry and fish.

Hints:
You can deep-fry the leaves and use them as a garnish.

In addition, dried sage leaves can be made into tea. Bring as many cups of water as you desire to a rolling boil in a teapot. Add 1-2 teaspoons of sage per cup to the teapot. Cover, and let the mixture stand for a few minutes. Sweeten with honey as desired. My mother gave the kids this tea whenever we had a sore throat.

Thyme (*Thimari*)
Thyme is a major culinary herb in Europe as well as in Greece. In Greece this herb grows abundantly in the wild on islands, and has a very strong smell. It shines in slow-cooked casseroles or sprinkled over grilled meat, poultry and fish.

Hint:
It has been used for years to alleviate symptoms of the common cold. Simply steep the leaves in boiling water for five minutes. Strain, and sip when cool enough. A spoonful of honey and a dash of lemon will add flavors and nutrients.

"Herbs in Greece have been used for generations to flavor food and for medicinal purposes."

Fresh Ideas

"Locally Sourced", "Veggies Galore", "From Farm to Table", and "Farm Fresh" are popular phrases and trends because these vegetables and fruits provide savory ingredients for fresh healthy cuisine. Crisp veggies and juicy fruits offer numerous wholesome qualities, including a variety of vitamins and minerals in addition to the characteristic signs of freshness from bright, lively colors to distinctive fresh scents.

When you approach a farmstand, the aroma of just-cut flowers infuses the air enticing your sense of smell as the bright, vibrant colors from nearby vegetables arouse your senses. Bite one scrumptious sample of arugula and the flavors burst in your mouth igniting your palate. You know why you came.

Your nutrition easily benefits from low-calorie, antioxidant-rich vegetables, fruits and herbs. As examples, ripe peaches are rich in beta carotene; blueberries boast vitamin C; and fresh-picked corn is packed with folate. Grapefruit is a wonderful source of vitamins A and B5, potassium, folate, and fiber. Plus, it's packed with cancer-fighting lycopene.

Greece is full of outdoor markets brimming with fresh local vegetables, fruits and fish. Consumers and restaurant owners visit these treasured culinary mines daily to obtain the best ingredients for their meals while conversing with friends and colleagues. You'll find that the recipes in "Greek Cooking My Way" thrive on fresh produce resulting in numerous health benefits.

As an example, the recipe for "Edamame Hummus" (see page 37) calls for edamame, lemon, garlic, sesame tahini, cumin, thyme, basil and mint. Edamame's isoflavones help starve cancer while the high amount of vitamin C in lemons helps keep the immune system strong. The Allicin compound in garlic appears to keep carcinogens from affecting healthy colon cells, and cumin has the potential to slow the growth of stomach and cervical tumors. Cumin can also assist in digestion and skin health. Mint contains perillyl alcohol, which has been shown in the lab to stall the growth of liver, mammary and pancreatic tumors.

Another recipe, "Rockin' Ratatouille" (see page 155), is also packed with wholesome ingredients. Some of those are eggplant, zucchini, yellow squash, red bell pepper, and olive oil. An anthocyanin phytonutrient found in the eggplant skin called nasunin is a potent antioxidant and free radical scavenger that has been shown to protect cell membranes from damage. (For more information visit The World's Healthiest Foods, www.whfoods.com) The fiber in zucchini helps lower cholesterol and the phytonutrients in zucchini aid in prostate health. (For more information, visit www.healthdiaries.com/eatthis)

The "Braised Escarole with Black-eyed Beans" recipe (see page 151) calls for black-eyed beans, escarole, olive oil, shallots, garlic, red bell pepper and lemon. Each ingredient has health benefits. As examples, the beans lower colon cancer risk, help to control blood sugar, and are a great source of protein and minerals such as phosphorus and iron. Escarole is packed with vitamin C and vitamin A. Shallots are a rich source of flavonoid antioxidants, and help reduce cholesterol. (For more information, visit www.nutrition-and-you.com/shallots.html)

"Greek Cooking My Way" is packed with many more nutritious recipes, but where do you find a wide variety of delicious local, farm-grown fresh fruits, vegetables, natural meats or cheeses? Localharvest (www.localharvest.org) provides a list by state for farmstands, "pick your own" farms (U-Pick), farmers' markets, Community Supported Agriculture (CSA), and more. In addition, some of the most popular places to acquire fresh produce are described here with links to helpful websites. A more extensive list of websites can be found in The Ultimate Food Scout section (see page 214).

Farmstands (Roadside stands)

Farmstands boast in-season fresh produce and often feature homemade breads, soups, pickles, jams, jellies and flowers. Some include displays of delicious homemade foods which may even include organic salads, soups, coffees, teas, smoothies, yogurt and ice cream. They are found throughout the country, especially in summer and early fall.

"Pick Your Own" Farms (or U-pick)

Visiting a "pick your own" farm is a terrific way to get the freshest produce. In addition, you can give your children a hands-on experience in the food growing and harvesting process. They may even have the opportunity to converse with the farmer while fostering a better sense of community.

To find a "pick your own" farm near you, visit www.pickyourown.org (a more complete list of websites can be found under The Ultimate Food Scout on page 214).

Farmers' Markets

Farmers' markets are one of the oldest means of direct marketing by small farmers throughout the world who sell their products once or twice a week at a designated public place such as a park, blocked off street, or parking lot.

In the last ten years they have become a favorite distribution method for many farmers across the United States and a favorite for many discerning shoppers.

To find a farmers' market near you, visit Local Harvest's website, www.localharvest.org/farmers-markets.

Community Supported Agriculture and Subscription Food Services

For over 25 years, Community Supported Agriculture (CSA) or Community Shared Agriculture has evolved as a popular way for consumers to purchase a membership (share) of fresh local harvest of seasonal food directly from farmers. The dividends come in the form of a weekly portion of the vegetable/fruit harvest.

CSA's goal is to keep farmers in business so that people in your area will benefit from access to healthy, fresh foods and attractive recreation areas for families. The concept is to eat foods from farms that you can see and enjoy in your daily life.

At the beginning of the growing season CSA members buy a share of the anticipated harvest. Once harvesting begins, participants receive a box or sometimes bag of locally-grown, in-season shares of vegetables and fruit each week. Sometimes, CSAs also include herbs, honey, eggs, dairy products and meat.

Local Harvest's website, www.localharvest.org/csa, can help you locate a CSA farm near you. They have a comprehensive list of over 4000 CSA farms.

CSA members obtain numerous benefits in addition to ultra-fresh food. They may receive specialty ingredients that they cannot find on their own and learn about new ways of cooking. Often, they will be able to visit the farm and have the farmer show their children how vegetables are grown. Most farmers provide original recipes and convenient time-saving deliveries.

There are also private companies that provide a similar service throughout the year. Some of the most well-known private companies delivering fresh foods via a subscription are Blue Apron, Chef Day, Healthy Chef Creations, Hello Fresh, The Magic Kitchen, Plated and Peach Dish.

Personal Gardens

If you have the time and expertise, growing your own garden can yield very healthy produce and be rewarding not only for yourself but your children. For detailed gardening links that can help you start your own garden, visit the gardening category on The Ultimate Food Scout, page 214.

Chapter 2

Thirst Quenchers

The Mystic Mastic Mojito

Zafira, a good-looking female bartender, stocks the Fox restaurant cooler with wine. It's a late summer afternoon in Syros, Greece, but well before the normal rush of thirsty patrons.

Periklis, a Greek in his late twenties, stumbles through the bar's open door. Looking dejected, he plops himself on a barstool in front of the long granite bar uttering,

PERIKLIS
Zafira, when you get a chance, could I get a glass of the Domaine Sigalas. The 2011 Nychteri.

Zafira gives Periklis a surprised look. Bottles clank as she hunts for his rare request.

ZAFIRA
What's the occasion? You get a raise? And why are you here so early?

PERIKLIS
Well... No. I have a huge problem.

Zafira looks puzzled.

ZAFIRA
A problem? It's summer in Greece. How could anyone have a problem?

PERIKLIS
I have one last chance to get a date with Aphrodite.

ZAFIRA
What's your big hurry? She's in here all the time.

PERIKLIS
She won't give me the time of day.

ZAFIRA
Big deal. Just ask her out for dinner next weekend.

PERIKLIS
That's the problem. She's job interviewing in Paris on Monday.

ZAFIRA
Now, that does sound like a predicament... But, my hobby is match-making.

From across the room a gruff drunken customer blurts,

BAD-TEMPERED CUSTOMER
Forget it, Z. Nobody can fix up that creep.

Periklis' face turns beet red, but he says nothing.

ZAFIRA
You want to get thrown out of here again this week? Just watch... if you can stay awake that long.

BAD-TEMPERED CUSTOMER
(belligerent)
I'll be awake. This I gotta see.

PERIKLIS
(sheepishly)
Maybe I'll just go to a movie.

ZAFIRA
Forget that! Give it one more try.

Zafira scratches her head and then smiles at Periklis.

ZAFIRA
I got a crazy idea... I'm going to create a drink. One that possesses mystic powers. One sip, and she'll think she's in paradise. A real <u>Aphrodisiac</u>... Get it?

Periklis glares at Zafira.

PERIKLIS
What? How you going to do that?

Patrons start entering the bar. Some sit at tables waiting for dinner but a few come to the bar and need attention. Zafira is undeterred from succeeding in her mission.

ZAFIRA
I'm going to use Mastic liqueur. Ever heard of it?

PERIKLIS
Sure, but isn't that the stuff used to fix gastric problems?

ZAFIRA
Don't be a killjoy. It's used in many desserts.

PERIKLIS
You sure this will work? You're my last hope.

ZAFIRA
It'll taste great, and pack a punch. Be ready!

Zafira temporarily morphs into an angelic bartender.

ZAFIRA
(softly with rhythm)
I'll mix it into a mojito. It'll be mystic and mastic... "The Mystic Mastic Mojito!"

PERIKLIS
Have you flipped?

Just then Aphrodite enters the bar. Periklis' heart palpitates.

PERIKLIS
(shyly)
Oh wow. What am I going to do?

ZAFIRA
Smile dude. Watch me, and be cool.

Aphrodite sits at the far end of the bar but avoids looking at Periklis.

Zafira begins creating her fabrication by pouring ingredients into a blender. She liquidizes them and in a flash partially fills a glass, adds the remaining ingredients, and tops this with two basil leaves.

An impatient Aphrodite yells,

APHRODITE
Can I get a little service over...

Zafira slides the drink in front of Aphrodite.

APHRODITE
(perturbed)
...here. What's this?

ZAFIRA
The specialty of the house.

APHRODITE
I don't want this. Give me-

ZAFIRA
(determined)
Just try it. The man at the end of the bar bought it. I guarantee you'll like it or your dinner's free.

Aphrodite takes a sip.

APHRODITE
Hey, this is good... Really good.

ZAFIRA
Glad you like it.

APHRODITE
What's it called?

ZAFIRA
It's "The Mystic Mastic Mojito."

APHRODITE
Wow! How'd you come up with such a great recipe?

ZAFIRA
Oh, it's not mine. The guy at the end of the bar created it.

APHRODITE
Clever... make a couple more of those and send them over.

Aphrodite takes her drink and strolls to Periklis. Being prepared, Zafira already has enough left in her blender for two more drinks and delivers them to Periklis just as Aphrodite arrives.

ZAFIRA
Here's the two drinks you ordered, Aphrodite.

Periklis' eyes pop. Zafira winks at him.

An hour later, Periklis and Aphrodite leave together. Aphrodite's arm is wrapped around Periklis' waist.

ZAFIRA
Yes!

See recipe on page 27.

MauiTini

Prep Time: 15 Min **Cook Time:** 0 Min **Total Time:** 15 Min

Serves 1

This passionate cocktail explodes with the enticing combination of flavors from guava nectar, lime, rhubarb, vodka and gin. Its creation was inspired when I visited Maui and is very refreshing when enjoyed in the late afternoon while watching a Hawaiian sunset.

Amount & Ingredients

1½ ounces mango vodka
2 ounces Tanqueray gin
5 drops rhubarb bitters
1 ounce grenadine syrup
1½ ounces guava nectar
1 ounce lime juice
1 scoop of ice

Garnish:

1 sugar cane stick

Directions

1. Put ingredients into a shaker.
2. Shake 3-4 times.
3. Pour shaker contents into a martini glass through a strainer.

Tip

Rhubarb bitters can be found at most large liquor stores or online. Sugar cane sticks can also be found easily online.

Serving Suggestions

Place the sugar cane stick in the glass resting it vertically against the side of the glass. Also, you can always multiply the ingredients to fill a pitcher with this refreshing drink for parties.

Mile High Mary

Prep Time: 15 Min **Cook Time:** 0 Min **Total Time:** 15 Min

Serves 1

This delicious cocktail was inspired when I visited the beautiful Hawaiian Island, Maui. It integrates a Greek twist which is especially refreshing at parties.

Amount & Ingredients

2 ounces ouzo
2 ounces citrus vodka
4 ounces V8 juice
½ teaspoon celery salt
1 teaspoon Worcestershire sauce
4 dashes Tabasco sauce
1 tablespoon lime juice

Garnish:

1 thin celery stalk
1 lime slice
1 thyme string

Directions

1. In a shaker filled halfway with ice, add all the ingredients.
2. Shake 3-4 times and strain into a tall glass.
3. Add the garnish.

Tip

In summer, you can make tomato juice in a juicer, and substitute the extract for the V8.

Serving Suggestions

You can multiply the ingredients to fill a pitcher for parties.

Mystic Mastic Mojito

The Greek Mojito

Prep Time: 10 Min **Cook Time:** 0 Min **Total Time:** 10 Min

Serves 1

If you love a mojito, you are going to really enjoy this Greek version. It's refreshing and promotes good digestion. See its story on page 19.

Mastika is the natural resin of a tree which grows on the Aegean island of Chios, Greece.

Amount & Ingredients

- ¼ cup mastic liqueur (such as Mastika Liqueur)
- 1 teaspoon sugar
- ¼ cup lemon juice
- 6 basil leaves
- 2 tablespoons crushed ice
- soda water

Directions

1. In a blender, add the mastic liqueur, sugar, lemon juice and 4 basil leaves.
2. Liquidize the above ingredients.
3. Add crushed ice to a tall glass.
4. Pour the liquidized ingredients into the glass.
5. Top the ingredients with soda water.
6. Garnish with 2 basil leaves.

Tip

This beverage is perfect as a pre-dinner drink, as well as after dinner since mastic is known for its soothing gastric qualities.

Serving Suggestions

This drink is best served and wonderful in chilled, tall glasses on a hot summer day.

Ouzorita

The Greek Margarita

Prep Time: 10 Min **Cook Time:** 0 Min **Total Time:** 10 Min

Serves 1

This is a strong and refreshing alternative to the traditional margarita, which gets its zip from the Greek aperitif, ouzo.

Amount & Ingredients

- 1 teaspoon crushed anise seed
- 2 teaspoons kosher Morton Iodized Salt
- 1 ounce ouzo
- 1 ounce tequila
- ¼ cup Cointreau liqueur
- 1 tablespoon honey
- ¼ cup lime juice
- 1 lime rind twist
- ½ cup crushed ice for serving

Directions

1. Mix the crushed anise seeds with salt and spread evenly on a plate.
2. Rub the outside rim of the margarita glass with a lime slice and dip the glass lightly onto a plate containing the salt mixture to coat the rim.
3. Combine ouzo, tequila, Cointreau, honey and lime juice in a blender until mixed.
4. Place the crushed ice into the margarita glass.
5. Pour the blender mixture into the margarita glass over the crushed ice.
6. Add a lime twist to the top of the mixture.

Tip

Instead of using ouzo you can use tsipouro which is a pomace brandy. It's a strong distilled spirit containing 40-45% alcohol by volume and is produced from the residue of the wine press. It comes in two types: pure or anise-flavored.

In Greece, it is tradition to be offered a tsipouro when visiting the home of friends.

Serving Suggestions

Yiasou (Cheers)!!!

AÑEJO
PATRÓN

Rena's Limoncello

An Aromatic Aperitif from the Mediterranean

Prep Time: 2 Weeks **Cook Time:** 15 Min **Total Time:** 2 Weeks

Yields 8 Cups

This smooth and sweet aperitif is characterized by an intense lemon flavor. It's considered to be the national drink of Italy and is often made using lemons from the Amalfi Coast where Sorrento lemons are plentiful. It can be sipped on its own, mixed into sparkling water, or shaken into cocktails. The taste ranges from very sweet to super tart or citrusy depending on the recipe used.

The recipe included here was given to me by my cousin, Rena. Lemon trees flourish in her garden in Syros, Greece, so it's always a treat for me to visit her and sip her heavenly creation.

Amount & Ingredients

10	organic lemons with thick skins
1	bottle 750ml tsipouro or vodka
3	cups white sugar
4	cups water

Directions

1. Wash lemons with a vegetable brush. Pat dry with a paper towel.
2. With a potato peeler remove the lemon skin. Do not include the white part because it's bitter and will spoil the drink. With a small sharp knife, remove any white parts from the skin and discard.
3. Place the lemon skins in a large glass bottle or jar.
4. Pour tsipouro or vodka over the skins and cover the bottle. Let it infuse for 1 week at room temperature.
5. After a week has passed, combine sugar and water in a large sauce pan over medium heat. Cook for 10-15 minutes, and let cool.
6. Pour the syrup mixture over the lemon mixture. Cover and let it stand for 1 week more.
7. Strain the limoncello through a very fine mesh strainer. Discard the skins.
8. Pour limoncello into glass bottles and seal with a cork. Let the mixture age for 4 days in the refrigerator. Then, store the bottles in the freezer.

Tip

Tsipouro can be found online or through major liquor vendors.

Serving Suggestions

Serve limoncello ice cold in vodka or shot glasses. You can drizzle limoncello on ice cream, a fruit salad or fresh strawberries.

Chapter 3

Preludes / Mezze

The Peace Pie

White homes and buildings with turquoise-domed roofs adorn the Santorini hillside, the southernmost member of the Cyclades group of Greek islands. The current horseshoe-shaped landmass was created by a violent volcanic eruption 3,600 years ago.

It's a beautiful clear late spring afternoon with the sun reflecting off the turquoise Aegean waters.

A young boy, Markos, carrying his school books, easily jogs up the cobblestone path that has steep drop-offs on each side. In his rush, however, he bumps one of the tourist-carrying donkeys. The donkey turns its head back and snorts,

HEE - HAW!

The startled rider, a male tourist, blasts,

TOURIST
What're you trying to do? Get me killed?

MARKOS
Sorry sir. I gotta get home quick.

Soon Markos sprints up a zigzag path past restaurants each cooking their own specialty. Wondrous aromas permeate the air. He darts up to his austere home and bursts through the kitchen entrance. His composed older sister, Korinna, who's just opening the door of an old-fashioned stove, wheels around asserting,

KORINNA
Wow. You're really worked up.

MARKOS
I got school trouble.

KORINNA
Oh, come on. How bad could that be?

MARKOS
I can't figure out fractions, and I got a civics report due.

KORINNA
Relax. I think I have something that can really help you.

Marcos gives his sister a questioning look.

MARKOS
How could you possibly help me?

KORINNA
I've got *Kremidopitas*, onion pies, in the oven.

MARKOS
We'll I'm hungry, but what about the fractions?

Korinna pulls a *Kremidopita* pie from the oven, and cuts it into four equal parts.

KORINNA
We have four parts, and each is one-fourth of the pie.

Korinna then divides the pie into eight equal parts.

KORINNA
Now each part is one-eighth. You get it?

MARKOS
Can I have a piece of pie?

Korinna removes a small slice, and serves it to Markos who eats so quickly he almost inhales the slice.

MARKOS
That was tasty, but I'm not too good with thirds.

KORINNA
No problem.

Korinna retrieves another steaming pie from the oven, and slices it into thirds.

KORINNA
You see each piece is one-third.

MARKOS
I'll take one of those thirds.

KORINNA
(frustrated and yelling)
Wait a second. You know your fractions. You're just trying to get more pie... Mom!

Markos holds the last pie up. It looks like a peace symbol.

MARKOS
Don't call mom. Peace... Please!

See recipe on page 49.

Edamame Hummus

Prep Time: 15 Min **Cook Time:** 2 Min **Total Time:** 17 Min

Serves 20

This healthy light *mezze* is easy to make and a gratifying beginning to a memorable meal.

Amount & Ingredients

- 2 cups frozen, shelled edamame
- 1 cup lemon juice
- 1 tablespoon lemon zest
- 2 garlic cloves chopped
- 2 tablespoons sesame tahini
- 1 teaspoon cumin
- 1 teaspoon salt
- 1 teaspoon wasabi powder
- 2 tablespoons chopped basil leaves
- 1 teaspoon dry thyme
- 2 tablespoons chopped mint leaves
- ½ cup olive oil

Garnish (for dipping):

- 4 cups fresh vegetables sliced such as carrot (or celery) sticks, cauliflower, and cucumber slices
- 20 crostinis

Directions

1. Put the frozen edamame into a microwave safe dish.
2. Cover with plastic wrap and cook on high for 2 minutes.
3. Remove the edamame from the microwave and let them stand for a few minutes to cool.
4. Put all the ingredients into a food processor and process until smooth.
5. If the mixture is too thick, add some water and blend for a few more seconds.

Serving Suggestions

Serve with fresh vegetables and/or crostinis nicely arranged around the hummus on a serving plate.

Eggplant Mustard Batons

Prep Time: 25 Min **Cook Time:** 15 Min **Total Time:** 40 Min

Serves about 24 pieces

The moisture of the eggplant enhanced by the spice of the mustard makes this appetizer an excellent drink accompaniment.

Amount & Ingredients

- 2 sheets frozen puff pastry thawed in the refrigerator
- 1 medium eggplant, skin off, cut into thin slices
- ¼ cup Kalamata pitted olives cut into thin slices
- 4 tablespoons Dijon mustard
- ½ cup Gruyere cheese, grated divided in half
- 3 tablespoons Parmesan cheese, grated
- 1 egg beaten with 1 tablespoon of water

Directions

1. Preheat the oven to 400°F.
2. Generously salt the eggplant and let it drain in a colander for 15-20 minutes.
3. Rinse the eggplant under cold running water and pat dry with paper towels.
4. Place the eggplant in a single layer on a baking sheet. Brush both sides liberally with olive oil.
5. Bake the eggplant for 15 minutes or until tender.
6. Line 2 baking sheets with parchment paper.
7. On a lightly floured surface, roll out one sheet of pastry into a rectangle about 12 x 16 inches.
8. Brush mustard over the pastry evenly. Spread the baked eggplant, olives and half the Gruyere cheese over the mustard.
9. Place on top the second sheet of puff pastry and pat with your hands.
10. Using a sharp knife, trim the edges of the dough.
11. Cut pastry into 1 x 6 inch strips (batons).
12. Spread the batons out evenly on the prepared sheet pan so they're not touching each other.
13. Brush the tops lightly with the egg wash and dust evenly with Gruyere and Parmesan cheese.
14. Bake batons in the oven for 15-20 minutes until puffed and golden.
15. Let the batons rest a few minutes before serving.

Tip You can prepare the batons early and refrigerate them until ready to bake.

Serving Suggestions Serve the batons warm or at room temperature.

Grilled Anaheim Peppers

Stuffed with Feta and Yogurt

Prep Time: 15 Min **Cook Time:** 10-11 Min **Total Time:** 25-26 Min

Serves 4

Peppers are perfect little vessels to hold a variety of stuffings such as this zesty combination of feta, yogurt, parsley, mint and lemon. In Greece this flavorful dish is often eaten while drinking ouzo.

Amount & Ingredients

- 4 Anaheim or Fresno peppers
- 1 cup crumbled feta cheese
- 1 tablespoon olive oil
- ¼ cup Greek yogurt
- 1 teaspoon fresh chopped parsley
- 1 teaspoon fresh chopped mint leaves
- ½ teaspoon lemon zest
- 2 egg yolks
- 1 tablespoon grated Parmesan cheese
- 1 tablespoon bread crumbs
- ½ teaspoon salt
- ¼ teaspoon black pepper freshly ground
- ¼ teaspoon red pepper flakes

Directions

1. Preheat the broiler to high.
2. Put peppers on a baking sheet.
3. Broil the peppers, turning once (2-3 minutes) until just soft (about 5-6 minutes).
4. Transfer the peppers to a rack and let cool.
5. In a food processor, put feta, oil, yogurt, parsley, mint, lemon zest and egg yolks. Mix until all ingredients are incorporated.
6. Salt to taste and add red pepper flakes.
7. Put peppers back onto the baking sheet.
8. Make a length-wise cut from the stem to the tip of each pepper.
9. Scoop out the seeds and ribs. Stuff each pepper with some feta filling.
10. In a small bowl, mix Parmesan and bread crumbs. Sprinkle this on top of the peppers.
11. Put the peppers back in the broiler and broil until the cheese is golden and bubbly (about 5 minutes).

Tip

You can try other varieties of peppers. In Greece the sweet Florina peppers are used.

Serving Suggestions

Serve each pepper hot with a small crostini bread.

Kickin' Chicken Liver Pâté

Prep Time: 15 Min | Cook Time: 15 Min | Total Time: 30 Min

Yields 3-4 ramekins

This silky-smooth pâté is inexpensive and simple to make.

It's a superb appetizer at a dinner party. Plus, it can be a light dinner or a sandwich spread. Also, it's a great starter for a holiday party and takes only a half-hour to prepare. Although it can be eaten the day it's made, it's more flavorful when made 1-2 days ahead.

Amount & Ingredients

- 1 pound chicken livers, cleaned
- ½ pound bacon roughly chopped
- 1 large onion roughly chopped
- ½ cup butter
- 3 bay leaves
- 1 teaspoon oregano
- 1 teaspoon thyme
- 1 teaspoon salt
- ½ teaspoon black pepper freshly ground
- 4 garlic cloves
- ⅓ cup brandy
- ½ cup heavy cream
- 2 tablespoons parsley chopped

Caramelized Onions:

- 2 onions sliced
- 1 tablespoon olive oil
- 2 tablespoons balsamic vinegar
- ½ teaspoon salt
- ¼ teaspoon black pepper freshly ground

Directions

1. Trim any fat or connective tissue from the livers and pat the livers dry.
2. In a large sauté pan over medium heat, add bacon, onion, butter and a bay leaf. Sauté about 10 minutes being careful to not burn.
3. Add the livers, spacing them apart in the pan so they brown evenly.
4. Sprinkle with oregano, thyme, salt and pepper.
5. When one side browns, flip the livers. Add garlic and sauté for 1 minute.
6. Remove pan from heat. Add brandy and replace pan on heat to simmer down the brandy (about 2 minutes).
7. Remove the bay leaf and discard.
8. Put the liver mixture into a food processor. Blend for 3-4 minutes. Add parsley and cream. Purée until very smooth. Taste for salt and pepper.
9. Pack the pâté into the ramekins or small bowls. Cover and refrigerate for at least 1 hour before serving.

To Prepare the Caramelized Onions:

1. In a large skillet, sauté 2 sliced onions with 1 tablespoon of olive oil, salt and pepper for 10 minutes.

2. Add 2 tablespoons balsamic vinegar and cook under low heat for 10 minutes more.

Tip

If you want to preserve the pâté for up to 1 month, pour a little clarified butter or unflavored gelatin on top to seal and refrigerate.

Serving Suggestions

Spread the pâté on crackers or toasted baguette slices. Place caramelized onions and sliced cornichons on top.

Marinated Gavros

Prep Time: 15 Min **Marinate Time:** 24 Hrs **Total Time:** 24 Hrs 15 Min

Serves 4

This tasty starter is the perfect preparatory dish for a great Greek meal. It's a small fish cured in salt, which is later served with a bit of olive oil as an appetizer.

Amount & Ingredients

- 1 pound gavros, cleaned
- 1 cup white wine vinegar
- ¾ cup extra virgin olive oil
- ⅓ cup fresh lemon juice
- 2 tablespoons flat-leaf parsley chopped
- 1 lemon sliced
- 2 garlic cloves, minced
- Kosher salt

For Serving:

- ¼ cup pitted and chopped Kalamata olives

Directions

1. Working with one gavro at a time, use a knife to remove the head.
2. Without piercing the fish all the way through, use the tip of the knife to loosen the spine and remove the bones from the flesh.
3. Rinse the cavity with 1 tablespoon of vinegar and transfer the deboned gavros to a small bowl.
4. Lightly season the cavity with salt.
5. Repeat steps 1-4 for the remaining fish.
6. Drain the gavros and arrange them in an 8 x 8 inch baking dish covered with lemon slices.
7. In a small bowl, whisk together the oil, lemon juice, parsley and garlic. Pour the marinade over the gavros massaging some of the marinade into the cavity of each fish.
8. Cover dish with plastic wrap and refrigerate overnight, turning the fish occasionally.

Tip

The gavros can stay in your refrigerator for 3-4 weeks.

Serving Suggestions

On a small serving plate, arrange the gavros in a circle (or side by side), heads facing inward. Surround the fish with sliced lemons and carefully place some Kalamata olives between the fish. Pour a little olive oil on top. Sprinkle with fresh parsley, and serve with bread or crostinis.

Mary's Olive Pâté

Prep Time: 15 Min | Cook Time: 0 Min | Total Time: 15 Min

Serves 20

This recipe was created by my sister, Mary, who lives in Greece. It's easy and a great addition for your next cocktail party.

Amount & Ingredients

1 cup pitted Kalamata olives
1 garlic clove
1 tablespoon sesame tahini
1 teaspoon Dijon style mustard
1 tablespoon lemon juice
¼ green apple
¼ teaspoon dry oregano
1 tablespoon extra virgin olive oil

Garnish:

20 crackers or crostini

Directions

1. Place all ingredients in a food processor.
2. Liquidize well until the mixture resembles a coarse paste.

Tip

This spread tastes best when made with high quality olives and olive oil.

Serving Suggestions

Pour the mixture into a small bowl and serve as a cocktail spread on a crisp cracker or a crostini. *Kali Orexi* ("Bon Appetite"), as we say in Greece.

Onion Pie

(Greek - *Kremidopita*)

Prep Time: 30 Min | **Cook Time:** 50 Min | **Total Time:** 1 Hr 20 Min

Serves 8

This is a delicious appetizer that is an excellent brunch mezze or can be a light dinner entrée.

Amount & Ingredients

Pastry Dough:

- 2 cups semolina flour
- 1 teaspoon salt
- ½ teaspoon baking soda powder
- ⅓ cup olive oil
- 1 cup room temperature water
- 1 teaspoon white wine vinegar

Filling:

- ½ pound (about 4) white onions halved and thinly sliced
- 2 teaspoons olive oil
- 1 teaspoon salt
- 2 tablespoons brandy or vermouth
- 2 tablespoons semolina flour
- 1 teaspoon fresh chopped thyme
- 1 teaspoon fresh chopped sage
- 4 lightly beaten eggs
- 1 cup crumbled feta cheese
- 1 cup grated Gruyere or Swiss cheese
- ½ teaspoon red pepper flakes

Directions

To Prepare the Dough:

1. In a medium bowl, mix flour, salt and baking soda powder.
2. Add olive oil, water and vinegar.
3. Knead the dough until it is very smooth (about 10-12 minutes).
4. Add more flour if needed (if dough sticks to your hands).
5. Make 4 equal balls.
6. Transfer the dough balls to an oiled bowl.
7. Cover the bowl with plastic wrap and let it stand for 1 hour at room temperature.

To Prepare the Filling:

1. In a large skillet over medium heat, add oil, onions and salt.
2. Toss the ingredients.
3. Cover the skillet and cook the ingredients for 10 minutes.
4. Lower the heat and stir the onions.
5. Cook them for 10-15 minutes more until the onions are soft and transparent.
6. Add brandy or vermouth and cook mixture for 5 minutes.
7. Add flour to absorb the liquids.
8. Add thyme and sage.
9. Remove skillet from heat.

10. Stir in the beaten eggs.
11. Combine the feta, Gruyere cheese and red pepper flakes with the onions and set aside.

To Prepare the Pie:

1. Preheat the oven to 350°F.
2. Lightly oil a 9-inch loose-bottom tart tin.
3. On a floured surface, place one of the dough balls.
4. Roll it into a circle 4 inches larger than the diameter of the pan.
5. Place the dough inside the pan leaving about 2 inches hanging over the pan's edge.
6. Brush the dough with olive oil.
7. Repeat the process with a second dough ball to create another layer.
8. Brush that dough ball also with olive oil.
9. Spread the filling evenly over the dough.
10. Repeat the rolling process for the third sheet, placing it over the filling and press it down gently.
11. Brush it with olive oil.
12. Roll out the last dough ball to form a slightly smaller piece placing it over the surface of the pie.
13. Join and fold in the bottom and top overhanging dough, rolling it around the perimeter of the pan to form a pretty rim.
14. Brush the top of the pie generously with olive oil.
15. Place the pie in the center of the oven and bake for about 40-50 minutes until the crust is golden and crisp.

Serving Suggestions

You can serve this as a side dish especially with roast beef. *Kremidopita* is also excellent when served as an item at a brunch buffet.

Smoked Eggplant Dip

Prep Time: 30 Min **Cook Time:** 20 Min **Total Time:** 50 Min

Serves 12

This is a fresh tasting dip. My grandmother baked the eggplant in an outside wood-burning oven but you can make it in your home barbeque.

Amount & Ingredients

- 2-3 medium eggplants
- 1 tablespoon lemon juice
- 1 teaspoon salt
- ⅓ cup finely chopped red onion
- 1 small seeded and minced jalapeño pepper
- 1 tablespoon finely chopped fresh basil
- 1 tablespoon finely chopped parsley
- 2 tablespoons chopped capers
- 1 large seeded and strained tomato cut into small cubes
- ½ cup cucumber cut into small cubes
- ⅓ cup olive oil
- 1 tablespoon lemon juice
- 1 tablespoon cider vinegar
- ¼ teaspoon salt
- ¼ teaspoon sugar
- ¼ teaspoon black pepper freshly ground

Directions

1. Position an oven rack approximately 6 inches from heat.
2. Preheat the broiler on high.
3. Line a baking sheet with foil. Place the eggplants onto the sheet, and poke a few holes to vent steam.
4. Broil each whole eggplant turning them with tongs every 5 minutes until the skin is charred.
5. To decide if an eggplant is ready (about 20 minutes), insert a knife into the stem area. If the knife enters easily, the eggplant is ready.
6. Transfer the eggplants to a cutting board.
7. When cool enough to handle, cut the eggplants in half length-wise and scrape the flesh into a fine sieve to strain all the liquid.
8. Put the lemon juice and salt on the strained eggplant to prevent discoloration.

To Prepare the Dressing:

1. Mix and combine well the olive oil, lemon, vinegar, salt, sugar and freshly ground pepper in a small bowl or jar.

To Prepare the Dip:

1. Transfer the strained eggplant flesh into a medium bowl.
2. Add onion, jalapeño, basil, parsley and capers.

3. Gently toss the mixture, and slowly add the dressing to incorporate it.
4. Cover and refrigerate for at least 1 hour or overnight.
5. Just before serving fold the cucumbers and cut tomatoes into the mixture, tossing gently.

Tip

You can use an outside grill for enhanced flavor in place of your oven.

Serving Suggestions

Serve in small bowls with fresh parsley sprinkled on top and toasted bread.

Syros Squash Blossoms

Prep Time: 45 Min **Cook Time:** 15 Min **Total Time:** 1 Hr

Serves 4-6

The delicate and elegant zucchini flower blooms mostly in summer. Lower latitude states such as Florida may have the blossoms during winter. In Greece, the blossoms are stuffed with rice and vegetables. My grandmother made her own Ricotta for the stuffing.

Amount & Ingredients

Stuffing:

- ¾ cup crumbled feta cheese
- ¾ cup Ricotta cheese
- 2 tablespoons grated Parmesan cheese
- 1 large egg
- 2 tablespoons finely chopped basil
- ½ cup fresh corn kernels
- ½ cup red bell pepper cut into small cubes
- 16 squash (zucchini) blossoms

Batter:

- ½ cup rice flour
- ½ cup all-purpose flour
- 1 teaspoon baking powder
- 1 teaspoon salt
- ½ teaspoon black pepper freshly ground
- 1 egg
- 2 cups vegetable oil

Directions

To Prepare the Stuffing:

1. In a medium bowl, mix feta, Ricotta, Parmesan and egg to combine.
2. Stir in basil, corn kernels and red pepper cubes. Season with salt and pepper.
3. Carefully spoon about 2 teaspoons of the stuffing mixture into each squash blossom.
4. Gently press the filling into the base of the flower. Cover the filling by folding inward each pedal of the flower to seal the top.
5. You can refrigerate the blossoms from 30 minutes to 2 hours.

To Prepare the Batter:

1. In a medium bowl, mix the rice flour, all-purpose flour, baking powder, salt and pepper.
2. Whisk the egg with ½ cup of water and add it to the flour mixture. If needed add up to ¼ cup of additional water to make a thinner batter.
3. Let the batter sit for 15 minutes.
4. Heat the oil in a large sauté pan until it reaches 375°F.
5. Holding each squash blossom by the stem dip each into the batter making sure to coat completely. Let any excess batter drip off.

6. Place the blossoms into the hot oil in batches of 4–5 and fry turning them to brown evenly until golden brown (approximately 1-2 minutes).
7. Remove the blossoms from the pan and place them on a paper towel to drain.

Tip

It's best to pick the blossoms early in the morning so they are open. If you purchase closed blossoms, be sure to open them gently and check for insects.

Serving Suggestions

Place the blossoms attractively in a circle over a platter of baby arugula. Serve the blossoms with marinara sauce or ranch dressing.

Trout Mousse

with Smoked Salmon

Prep Time: 30 Min   Cook Time: 4 Hrs   Total Time: 4 Hrs 30 Min

Serves 6

Trout mousse covered with a thin layer of smoked salmon is simple, and quick to make. It's a wonderful combination of flaked fish, horseradish, yogurt and lemon.

This satisfying dish was always very popular in my restaurants.

Amount & Ingredients

- 2 smoked trout filets – discard skin and bones and cut filet into small pieces
- 2 tablespoons mayonnaise
- 2 tablespoons unflavored Greek yogurt
- 4 tablespoons heavy cream beaten
- 1 tablespoon horseradish sauce
- 2 tablespoons lemon juice
- 1 teaspoon lemon zest
- 2 tablespoons unflavored gelatin dissolved in 2 tablespoons cold water
- 4 tablespoons ouzo or gin
- 2 tablespoons fresh dill chopped
- ½ pound smoked salmon
- pinch of salt and pepper

Directions

1. In a soufflé dish or in muffin cups, layer the smoked salmon at the bottom and around the sides.
2. In a bowl, mix the mayonnaise, yogurt, horseradish, lemon juice, lemon zest and dissolved gelatin.
3. Add the smoked trout, chopped dill, ouzo (or gin) and beaten cream.
4. Mix the ingredients gently with a rubber spatula and spoon the mixture into the prepared dish. Refrigerate for 4-6 hours.
5. To unmold the mousse, run a knife around the edge of mold and carefully turn it over on the serving plate.

Tip

For a real Greek specialty, substitute ouzo in place of gin.
You can substitute fresh smoked salmon for the trout as a variation.

Serving Suggestions

Serve cold on a bed of finely chopped lettuce with slices of hard-boiled egg sprinkled with dill and smoked paprika.

Two-way Stuffed Cherry Tomatoes

Prep Time: 20 Min **Cook Time:** 0 Min **Total Time:** 20 Min

Yields 36 Stuffed Tomatoes

Two different stuffings – one based on Kalamata olives and the other on creamy feta cheese – make for a fresh, light and delectable appetizer.

Amount & Ingredients

36 medium cherry tomatoes

Olive Stuffing:

- 4 boned and skinned anchovies in olive oil, well drained
- 1 cup pitted Kalamata olives
- 1 tablespoon chopped celery leaves
- 2 gherkins, chopped
- ¼ teaspoon cayenne pepper

Cheese Stuffing:

- ¾ cup feta cheese
- ¾ cup Ricotta cheese
- 1 tablespoon mint
- 1 tablespoon basil
- 1 garlic clove
- ½ teaspoon white pepper
- ½ teaspoon salt

Directions

1. Cut a small cap off the top of each tomato.
2. With a small scoop or your finger, remove all the pulp.
3. Invert the hollowed-out tomatoes and place them on a plate to drain.

To Prepare the Olive Stuffing:

1. In a food processor, place the anchovies, olives, celery, gherkins and cayenne. Process until the ingredients form a coarse paste.
2. Using a small spoon, fill 18 of the tomatoes with the olive stuffing.

To Prepare the Cheese Stuffing:

1. In a food processor, place feta, Ricotta, basil, mint, garlic, white pepper and salt. Briefly process to a creamy texture.
2. Using a small spoon or a piping bag, fill the remaining 18 tomatoes with the cheese stuffing.

Tip

The fillings are excellent as a dip with crudité.

Serving Suggestions

After filling the tomatoes, refrigerate them until time to use.

Chapter 4

Soups and Salads

In Every Grey Cloud There's a Culinary Savior

We're in Miss Skordas' grammar school writing class on the Greek island of Mikonos. It's an old-fashioned classroom with wooden desks on the Friday before the 1981 Christmas break. Snow-frosted windows adorn the room which bustles with festive activity.

Eleven-year-old Agapi and her twelve-year-old brother, Stefanos, listen intently to their teacher. She's in her late fifties, and has a caustic demeanor that demands perfection.

MISS SKORDAS
(sternly)
Class...

Nereus, the class bully, however, stares out the window not paying attention. Miss Skordas glares at Nereus, and simultaneously slaps her meter-long ruler on her desk.

WHAM!

MISS SKORDAS
... Remember, your term papers are due the first Monday after we get back from Christmas holiday and they must be a story that taught you a life lesson. Those of you who don't do well will be held back a grade... Any questions?

The other class members stare at each other trembling.

A few hours later school lets out. It's a crisp afternoon with the sky just starting to drizzle a fine mist that saturates the walkways. Stefanos carries Agapi's books as the two saunter home. Their treasured writing work is amongst this eclectic collection.

STEFANOS
How the heck we gonna come up with a couple of stories by next week? We're in big trouble.

AGAPI
Don't lose sleep. We'll find a way.

STEFANOS
But, we should take a different route home.

AGAPI
Come on, Stefanos. Let's not go out of our way. I'm in a hurry to start our homework.

As they walk down a narrow marble pathway bordered by a variety of shops, Nereus pops out from an alley.

AGAPI
Oh no!

STEFANOS
Hey, Nereus. What are you doing around here?

NEREUS
Just waiting for you, twerp.

He darts up to a startled Stefanos, and yanks on a corner of the stack of books Stefanos is carrying. Books and papers fly in a hundred directions scattering over the wet pavement.

NEREUS
Try getting your report in on time now.

Agapi and Stefanos rush to their wet papers trying to minimize the damage.

STEFANOS
Nereus, you jerk.

NEREUS
Next time I see you I'm gonna make your face into a culinary masterpiece... a "pound cake."

Nereus laughs and slithers back into the alley out of sight.

The next day, Agapi and Stefanos rush into their kitchen. It's filled with olive and fruit preserve jars. A wood-burning stove warms the air and dries several dozen school papers that are pinned to a clothesline in the background. The smell of baking bread, a Mikonos tradition, permeates the air.

Marina, their mother, wearing a white apron with a large Greek flag on it, chops vegetables.

AGAPI
Mom, while our papers are drying can Stefanos and I go to the Christmas festival at the town square? It's-

STEFANOS
Are you crazy. Nereus might be around.

Through the kitchen window the sky turns grey, and...

BOOM!

...A lightning bolt strikes the ground a mile away. Rain pelts the house in a torrential downpour as the wind violently erupts.

MARINA
That's some rain storm. Looks like you'll have to stay here. You can help me prepare the Christmas soup, Vegetable Borscht with Chicken, for our Christmas lunch party.

AGAPI
But, we'll miss the festival!

MARINA
Our guests will be here for lunch. How 'bout getting into the Christmas spirit. Do something for others?

STEFANOS
Yeah, who needs the festival anyway.

MARINA
It's important to have the spirit, especially this time of year.

Marina ties matching aprons on her children and the three scurry around the kitchen's wooden table chopping beets, garlic, onions, potatoes, cabbage and celery. They're having fun as a family. When they add the ingredients, their soup begins its transformation into a heart-warming amalgamation, spewing tempting aromas which saturate the room.

Marina smiles and gives her children a nod of approval. Agapi and Stefanos grin, knowing they've done the right thing.

Soon the guests and family arrive soaked. However, when they sniff the wonderful aromas that have filled the house, their eyes open wide visualizing the culinary creations to come. Their hearts warm.

Agapi and Stefanos share the serving responsibilities. The guests love the soup and ask for refills. When Agapi returns to the kitchen, she peers out the window. Through the downpour she notices Nereus, drenched and wind beaten.

AGAPI
Look at that. It's Nereus. He's walking alone out in the storm.

Agapi throws on a coat and hat as she sprints out the door.

STEFANOS
(yelling)
What? Are you crazy?

Agapi catches up to Nereus blurting,

AGAPI
Nereus what are doing out in the rain all alone?

NEREUS
What the heck do you care?

AGAPI
It's the Christmas season. Why aren't you with your family?

NEREUS
I got no family. My parents... Aw forget it.

AGAPI
Come in our house, and have some hot soup.

A few minutes later Nereus is seated at the kitchen table wolfing down the Christmas soup.

NEREUS
That's very tasty. Really warms me up. Who made it?

AGAPI
Stefanos and I did.

Nereus gives Agapi and Stefanos a mean look. As they start to shake, he articulates,

NEREUS
I used to get straight A's in creative writing at my previous school... Well, that's before they kicked me out for fighting...

Nereus grins.

NEREUS
...Maybe I could help you with your writing projects.

See recipe on page 79.

Beetroot, Yogurt and Walnut
Salad

Prep Time: 20 Min   **Cook Time:** 0 Min   **Total Time:** 20 Min

Serves 8

This colorful, healthy and tasty dish can be served nicely either as a buffet item or dinner salad.

Amount & Ingredients

- 1 pound fresh beetroots
- 1 cup of grated carrots
- 2 tablespoons lemon juice
- 1 tablespoon lemon zest
- 1 teaspoon salt
- 1 cup thick Greek yogurt
- ½ cup mayonnaise
- 1 tablespoon horseradish sauce
- 1 clove crushed garlic
- ½ cup shredded green apple
- 1 tablespoon olive oil
- 2 tablespoons coarsely chopped walnuts
- 3 cups fresh arugula

Garnish:

- 1 tablespoon chopped parsley
- ¼ apple thinly sliced

Directions

1. Thoroughly wash the beetroots and peel them like a potato.
2. Shred the beetroot and place the pieces in a bowl with carrots, lemon and salt.

To Prepare the Yogurt:

1. In a bowl, blend the yogurt, mayonnaise, horseradish, garlic, shredded apple and olive oil.
2. Gently mix them to combine.
3. Add the shredded beetroots to the yogurt mixture.
4. Add the chopped walnuts and gently mix.

To Prepare the Salad:

1. Attractively arrange the arugula on a large serving plate.
2. Place the yogurt mixture in the center of the arugula.

Tip

You also can add half a cup of golden raisins.

Serving Suggestions

Garnish the salad with parsley and thin slices of green apple.

Butternut Squash

Soup

Prep Time: 15 Min **Cook Time:** 50 Min **Total Time:** 1 Hr 5 Min

Serves 6

This is a tasty and filing soup with few calories.

Amount & Ingredients

- 2 tablespoons olive oil
- 1 cup onions chopped into small cubes
- 1 cup carrots chopped into small cubes
- 2 garlic cloves minced
- 1 jalapeño seeded and finely chopped
- 1 cup potato, peeled and cut into small cubes
- 6 cups butternut squash
- ½ cup orange and green peppers cut into small cubes
- 1 teaspoon garam masala
- 1 teaspoon curry powder
- 6 cups homemade vegetable or chicken stock

Garnish:

- 1 cup baby arugula
- 2 tablespoons chopped parsley

Directions

1. In a large saucepan over medium heat, add the oil and onion. Sauté for 2 minutes.
2. Add garlic and sauté for 1 minute.
3. Meanwhile, with a sharp knife peel the butternut squash and scoop out the seeds. Cut the flesh into small cubes.
4. Add the squash, potatoes, carrots, jalapeño and peppers to the saucepan. Cook for another 2 minutes.
5. Add the garam masala and curry. Stir and cook for 1 minute.
6. Pour in the stock. Bring to a boil and cook over low heat for about 45 minutes, uncovered, stirring every 10 minutes.
7. Put ⅔ of the stock mixture into a food processor and liquidize.
8. Combine the liquidized mixture with the remaining stock.
9. Cook 2-3 minutes more stirring occasionally.

Tip

If you prefer a smoother texture, the complete mixture can be liquidized.

If you want an easier way to chop your vegetables into small cubes, you can use a product such as the Vidalia Chop Wizard.

Serving Suggestions

Serve hot, garnished with some chopped parsley or arugula leaves.

Cauliflower and Broccoli

Rabes Soup

Prep Time: 15 Min   **Cook Time:** 20 Min   **Total Time:** 35 Min

Serves 4-6

This tasty and healthy vegetarian soup can be created from leftover broccoli rabes and cauliflower. Plus, it's a low calorie dish that can be served as a starter or an entrée.

Amount & Ingredients

- 2 tablespoons olive oil
- 1 cup onion chopped
- 2 garlic cloves minced
- 1 potato diced small
- 1 pound cauliflower – florets chopped
- 1 bunch broccoli rabes chopped
- 1 teaspoon dried oregano
- 1 teaspoon salt
- ½ teaspoon white pepper
- 5 cups water or vegetable stock
- ½ cup quinoa milk
- ½ cup Parmesan (crumbled blue cheese or cheddar cheese – optional)

Directions

1. Make sure your broccoli rabes are thoroughly washed.
2. In a sauce pan over medium heat, add olive oil and onion.
3. Cook, and stir for about 4 minutes until the onion is translucent.
4. Add garlic. Stir and cook for 15 seconds.
5. Add potatoes, cauliflower, broccoli rabes, salt and pepper. Sauté for 2-3 minutes.
6. Add water or stock and bring the mixture to a boil. Cover and reduce heat. Simmer for 15 minutes.
7. Put 3 cups of the mixture in a food processor and liquidize.
8. Return the liquidized mixture to the original ingredients and combine.
9. Taste for seasoning.

Tip

Using chicken stock instead of the vegetable stock creates a delicious alternative.

Serving Suggestions

Serve the soup hot with crackers or crostini. Add the cheese of your choice sprinkled on top or mixed in.

Chilled "Honey Do" Melon

Soup

Prep Time: 15 Min **Cook Time:** 1 Hr **Total Time:** 1 Hr 15 Min

Serves 2

This soup is a refreshing dish on a hot evening while dining under the stars. It's the perfect meal to persuade your "honey" to "do" a difficult task.

Amount & Ingredients

- 1 medium sized honeydew melon
- 1 garlic clove
- 1 skinned and seeded tomato
- 2 tablespoons balsamic vinegar
- 2 tablespoons olive oil
- ½ teaspoon salt
- ¼ teaspoon black pepper freshly ground
- 6 basil leaves
- 1 skinned and seeded tomato cut into small cubes

Garnish:

- 4 basil leaves
- 1 fresh vine leaf or other green leaf
- 1 tomato

Directions

1. Wash the melon. With a sharp knife, cut a zigzag pattern in the middle along the circumference.
2. Open the melon and discard the seeds.
3. With a melon baller or a mini scoop scrape 4-6 melon balls and place them in a small dish for later use.
4. Carefully scoop out the flesh of the melon and place it in a food processor or blender.
5. Add garlic, one tomato, balsamic vinegar, olive oil, salt, pepper and the six basil leaves to the blender and liquidize.
6. Store this mixture in a container in the refrigerator.
7. Put the empty melon shells into the freezer for about 1 hour.
8. Cut the second tomato into small cubes and roughly chop the basil.
9. Place the melon shells on a serving plate and fill them with the chilled blended mixture.
10. Garnish with the chopped tomato, melon balls and basil.

Tip

You can place a fresh vine leaf or any other green leaf under the melon half to enhance your presentation. If you would like the soup to be a lighter color, use white balsamic vinegar.

Serving Suggestions

If you don't want to use the melon half, you can serve the blended mixture in small glasses.

Farro Salad

with Baked Vegetables

Prep Time: 15 Min | Cook Time: 20 Min | Total Time: 35 Min

Serves 4

A healthy, low-calorie vegetarian salad that enhances seafood and poultry dishes.

Amount & Ingredients

Salad:

- 1 cup farro
- 1 green zucchini cut into small cubes
- 1 yellow zucchini cut into small cubes
- 1 red bell pepper stemmed, seeded and cut in cubes
- 1 cup mushrooms cut into cubes
- 1 cup onion cut into cubes
- 2 garlic cloves finely chopped
- ½ teaspoon black pepper freshly ground
- 1 teaspoon salt
- 2 tablespoons basil roughly chopped
- 2 tablespoons parsley chopped

Dressing:

- ¼ cup apple cider vinegar
- ¼ cup lemon juice
- 1 teaspoon lemon zest
- 1 teaspoon Dijon mustard
- 1 garlic clove minced
- ½ cup olive oil
- ½ teaspoon salt
- ¼ teaspoon black pepper freshly ground

Directions

1. Preheat oven to 400°F.
2. Cook the farro as the label directs.
3. Drain farro, transfer to a bowl and toss with a teaspoon of olive oil.
4. Spray a roasting pan with olive oil cooking spray.
5. In the prepared pan, spread in a single layer the zucchini, peppers, mushrooms, onion, garlic, salt and pepper.
6. Roast the vegetables for 20 minutes.
7. Meanwhile, prepare the dressing in a small bowl by mixing the mustard, apple cider vinegar, lemon juice, lemon zest, salt and pepper.
8. Mix the farro, baked vegetables, basil and parsley.
9. Pour the dressing over the farro mixture and toss.

Tip

If you would like some protein, you can add a grilled chicken breast or salmon filet. You may augment this dish with fresh arugula and cherry tomatoes for additional flavor and color.

Serving Suggestions

Serve warm or room temperature with fresh cut parsley and basil on top.

Filet Mignon Salad

with Arugula

Prep Time: 10 Min **Cook Time:** 10 Min **Total Time:** 20 Min

Serves 2

This flavorful combination is a delectable quick lite lunch or dinner. The meat juices mingle with the spice of the arugula to create an enticing taste. It's not only satisfying but will help keep you fit.

Amount & Ingredients

Salad:

- 2 tablespoons olive oil
- 2 medium shallots sliced
- ¾ pound filet mignon cut into ½-inch thick slices
- ½ cup sweet red pepper roasted and cut into thin strips
- 1 teaspoon salt
- ½ teaspoon black pepper freshly ground
- 1 tablespoon aged balsamic vinegar
- 2 cups fresh baby arugula
- 10 Belgium endive leaves sliced medium thick
- 2 radishes thinly sliced
- 6 yellow and red cherry tomatoes cut in half

Dressing:

- ½ teaspoon Dijon mustard
- 1 tablespoon balsamic vinegar
- 1 teaspoon apple cider vinegar
- ¼ cup extra virgin olive or avocado oil
- ⅓ teaspoon salt
- ⅛ teaspoon white pepper

Directions

1. Heat the olive oil in a cast iron skillet over high heat.
2. Place the shallots in the skillet and sauté for 2-3 minutes.
3. Add the filet mignon to the skillet and sauté for 4-5 minutes.
4. Add the red pepper strips, balsamic vinegar, salt and pepper. Sauté for 1-2 minutes more. Remove from heat.
5. In a medium bowl, combine the endive, arugula, radishes and tomatoes.
6. In a small bowl, whisk the mustard, vinegars, olive oil, salt and pepper.
7. Pour the dressing over the endive / arugula mixture and toss it until the dressing evenly coats the greens.
8. Transfer the salad to a platter. Top the salad with the filet and red pepper mixture. Drizzle some skillet juices over the salad.

Tip

You can make this salad with any cut of steak, chicken or turkey.

Serving Suggestions

This salad should be served warm. A garlic crostini on the side adds an addictive touch.

Lentil Vegetable Soup

Prep Time: 15 Min   Cook Time: 45 Hr   Total Time: 1 Hr

Serves 8-10

A delicious hearty vegetable bean soup that's consumed throughout the Mediterranean. This nutritious dish is a good source of protein, dietary fiber, iron and potassium. It can be offered as an entrée as well as a side.

Amount & Ingredients

- 16 ounces dried lentils
- 1 tablespoon olive oil
- 1 large onion chopped
- 4 garlic cloves chopped
- 2 cups cauliflower chopped
- 2 leeks, white and green parts only, halved, washed carefully, and chopped
- 2 large carrots, peeled and chopped
- 3 celery stalks chopped
- 1 red bell pepper stemmed, seeded and chopped
- 2 bay leaves
- 1 tablespoon fresh thyme chopped
- 1 teaspoon cumin
- ¼ teaspoon cayenne pepper
- 1 large can (32 oz.) diced tomatoes with juice
- 8 cups water or low sodium vegetable broth
- 2 cups kale or Swiss chard chopped
- 1 teaspoon salt, or to taste

Directions

1. Sort the lentil beans discarding any stones or impurities.
2. Rinse the lentils in a wire mesh strainer.
3. Heat the oil in a heavy large pot over medium heat.
4. Sauté the onion for about 4 minutes.
5. Add the garlic and sauté for 30 seconds more.
6. Add leeks, carrots, pepper, celery, thyme, cumin, cayenne and bay leaves. Sauté for 1 minute.
7. Add the tomatoes, lentils, water (or vegetable broth), and simmer for 30 minutes.
8. Add the cauliflower and kale. Simmer another 15 minutes.

Tip

For additional protein you can add grilled chicken or roast turkey that has been sliced into thin strips.

Serving Suggestions

Serve hot with fresh bread or pitas. For increased flavor, sprinkle with crumbled feta.

Vegetable Borscht Soup

with Chicken

Prep Time: 15 Min | **Cook Time:** 40 Min | **Total Time:** 55 Min

Serves 6

This hearty soup will feed your soul and need for beets. It's a healthy way to get through a chilly fall or winter day by consuming a wonderfully satisfying soup. Especially since beets, this earthy root vegetable, are absolutely delicious.

My Ukrainian friend, a ballet dancer, stayed in my home and introduced me to this traditional regional soup. Over dinner we shared many culinary stories about our respective countries and developed a close bond.

Amount & Ingredients

- 2 tablespoons olive oil
- 1 yellow onion chopped into small cubes
- 2 garlic cloves finely chopped
- 4 cups thinly sliced green cabbage
- 2 medium russet potatoes peeled and shredded
- 3 medium beets peeled and shredded
- 2 medium carrots peeled and shredded
- 1 celery stalk chopped into small cubes
- 2 bay leaves
- 2 tablespoons red wine vinegar
- 2 tablespoons tomato paste
- 8 cups low sodium chicken broth
- 2 large skinless, boneless chicken breasts cut into ½ inch pieces
- 2 teaspoons salt
- ½ teaspoon freshly ground pepper

For Serving:

- ½ cup low fat sour cream
- 1 tablespoon horseradish
- 2 tablespoons chopped parsley

Directions

1. Heat the oil in a large soup pot over medium heat. Add onion and sauté for 5 minutes. Add garlic and sauté for 1 minute more. Add the cabbage, potatoes, beets, carrots, celery and bay leaf. Sauté for 8–10 minutes stirring occasionally.
2. Add red wine vinegar, tomato paste and chicken broth. Increase heat to medium-high. Bring to a boil. Cook for 15 minutes. Add chicken, salt and pepper. Reduce heat to medium low and simmer for 15-20 minutes more.
3. Check for seasoning.

Tip This soup can be made vegetarian. Also, you can supplement this soup when it is ready to be served by topping it with fresh shredded cabbage, carrots and beets.

Serving Suggestions In a small bowl, combine sour cream and horseradish. Ladle soup into bowls. Top it with the sour cream mixture and parsley.

Chapter 5

Ocean Chosen

The Blue Panther

It's a warm summer afternoon in Greece. Poppi and Antonios, two Greeks in their late twenties, drive along the countryside in a small egg-shaped Opal to the port city of Kalamata. The tiny tourist town is filled with energetic activity. Tourists flood the shops and taverns for one last chance to purchase a souvenir or drink.

HONK! HONK! HONK!

The harbor's sole cruise ship blasts its warning horn signifying its departure in twenty minutes. The town's tourists quickly return to their vessel. The boat departs and all shops close. However, Poppi and Antonios remain.

ANTONIOS
What happened? This just turned into a ghost town and I'm hungry.

POPPI
That's what happens when the boat leaves.

Antonios gazes around surveying the restaurants.

ANTONIOS
Look at these empty restaurants.

POPPI
Hey, check this one out.

Poppi gestures to an open air bistro that's on the pier with a tremendous view of the port and the upcoming sunset.

ANTONIOS
Wait a second. How do we know the fish is fresh?

POPPI
Come on! We have our choice of the best table in the house.

Poppi grabs Antonios by the arm and drags him to a great table with a fantastic view.

ANTONIOS
You sure the food's fresh?

POPPI
Don't worry. I've got things under control.

ANTONIOS
That's what you said when we got lost driving.

A summer breeze blows off the Aegean Sea swirling Poppi's hair as a young handsome waiter approaches their table.

WAITER
Good afternoon. Welcome to Monopolio. *Ti kanies* (How are you)?

POPPI
Kalaeime (Well).

WAITER
Let me tell you about our fresh fish specials.

POPPI
Hold on. Is it possible for me to see your fish?

WAITER
Of course.

Poppi stares at the waiter.

WAITER
(timidly)
Ah... Follow me.

Poppi and Antonios accompany the waiter across the street to Monopolio's kitchen. He points to several chilled drawers.

WAITER
Check these out. We have branzino, mussels, shrimp,-

Poppi pulls out the branzino drawer, looks a fish in the eye, and pushes on the skin.

POPPI
This one's very fresh. We'll take it. Can you grill it whole?

WAITER
Sure thing, ma'am.

Thirty minutes later the waiter brings a cast iron platter to the table with the grilled branzino steaming, still cooking in its own juices.

Antonios and Poppi's ravenous eyes widen as they immediately start devouring the fish.

ANTONIOS
Wow! This is the best restaurant fish I've ever eaten! How'd you know to pick it?

POPPI
My nickname isn't the Blue Panther for nothing!

Branzino à la Syros

(Greek – *Lavraki*)

Prep Time: 10 Min **Cook Time:** 30 Min **Total Time:** 40 Min

Serves 4

This fish, which ranges in size from one-and-a-half to three pounds, has a firm, white, delicate-flavored flesh. It's found frequently in Mediterranean countries such as Greece, Italy, and Spain where it is often grilled, roasted, poached, steamed, or braised whole.

Amount & Ingredients

- 4 branzino filets, ½ lb. each
- 2 teaspoons salt
- ½ teaspoon freshly ground black pepper
- 1 teaspoon dried thyme
- 1 teaspoon dried rosemary
- 1 teaspoon dried oregano
- 2 medium onions thinly sliced
- 2-3 lemons cut into thin slices, pits and ends discarded
- ½ cup of white wine
- 4 tablespoons olive oil
- 2 tablespoons chopped parsley

Directions

1. Preheat the oven to 425°F.
2. Season the filet with salt and pepper. Sprinkle with thyme, rosemary and oregano.
3. Place a layer of onions drizzled with 2 tablespoons of olive oil on a baking pan.
4. Place 1 layer of lemon slices on top of the onions, and bake them for 15 minutes.
5. Remove the pan from the oven. Place the branzino filet on top of the lemons, skin side up.
6. Pour the wine into the pan, and drizzle the fish with the remaining 2 tablespoons of olive oil.
7. Place the pan back into the oven, and bake for 15-20 minutes more until the fish is cooked through.

Tip

You can marinate the fish with herbs and olive oil. Leave it in the refrigerator for 1-2 hours before cooking.

Serving Suggestions

Place the fish on a platter. Arrange the onions and lemon around the outside. Sprinkle with parsley.

Eirini's Lobster Linguine

(Greek – *Astakomakaronada*)

Prep Time: 10 Min **Cook Time:** 20 Min **Total Time:** 30 Min

Serves 4-5

While free diving in Syros, Greece with my sister, Eirini, and collecting sea urchins, I caught a lobster. Eirini prepared the lobster using this recipe for an exciting dinner combining the thrill of summer with just the right trace of heat.

Amount & Ingredients

- 2 lobsters (1-1½ lbs. each)
- 12 ounces uncooked linguine
- 4 tablespoons olive oil
- 2 shallots finely sliced
- ½ teaspoon red pepper flakes crushed
- 1 teaspoon salt
- 2 large tomatoes skinned, seeded and chopped
- ⅓ cup dry white wine
- ½ teaspoon fennel seeds
- 1 teaspoon lemon zest
- 2 tablespoons parsley finely chopped

Directions

1. Ask the fishmonger at your fish market to split the live lobster in half lengthwise or do it yourself.
2. Remove and discard stomach sack located just behind eyes.
3. Heat olive oil in a large skillet over medium heat.
4. Sauté lobster cut side down for about 5 minutes.
5. Move the lobster to a large cutting board and let it cool slightly.
6. In the same skillet, sauté shallots, red pepper flakes, fennel seeds and salt for 1 minute.
7. Add chopped tomatoes and wine stirring often until tomatoes are soft and juicy (about 6-8 minutes). Turn heat off.
8. Carefully remove lobster meat from shells and cut into 1-inch pieces. Add lobster meat to tomato sauce.
9. Using a "lobster cracker", crack the claws and remove the meat. Carefully add this meat to the sauce.
10. You may keep the head for decoration.
11. Cook linguine in a large pot of boiling salted water stirring occasionally until "al dente."
12. Drain reserving 1 cup of pasta cooking liquid.
13. Add linguine and ½ cup reserve pasta cooking liquid to lobster tomato mixture. Use tongs to toss the pasta in the sauce. Cook for 2 minutes adding some more cooking liquid if needed to make the sauce juicier.

14. Check for seasoning.
15. Drizzle with a bit more olive oil.

Tip

If you cannot find someone to cut the lobster, you can steam it for 5 minutes, and then cut it.

For additional flavor, you can cook the lobster head with the linguine.

Serving Suggestions

Arrange the meat and claws on top. Sprinkle with lemon zest and parsley. Serve pasta warm.

Finikas Paella

with Seafood and Chicken

Prep Time: 20 Min **Cook Time:** 30 Min **Total Time:** 50 Min

Serves 6

Paella is widely regarded as Spain's national dish, although it is popular throughout the Mediterranean including Greece. This comfort food can be made with seafood, chicken, or a combination of both. The Spanish chorizo and saffron threads give a unique flavor to the rice (Bomba, Senia or Calasparra).

Finikas is a small port on the island of Syros, Greece where fishermen bring fresh seafood. The local farmers deliver vibrant vegetables and wholesome chicken, which allows nearby restaurants to prepare some of the finest paella.

Amount & Ingredients

- 3 links of Spanish chorizo chopped into ½ inch thick slices
- 1 pound chicken thighs, deboned and skin off
- 2 teaspoons salt
- 1 teaspoon pepper
- 1½ teaspoons saffron threads
- 12 large shrimps peeled, deveined and seasoned with salt and pepper
- 4 tablespoons extra virgin olive oil
- 1 medium onion cut into small cubes
- 3 garlic cloves, minced
- 1 cup white wine
- 1 15 oz. can whole tomatoes, drained, hand crushed, juice reserved
- 2 dried bay leaves
- ½ teaspoon thyme
- 20 mussels, cleaned and debearded
- 20 little neck clams, scrubbed and washed
- 6 scallops, chopped
- 3 small calamari, sliced into rings ¼ inch thick
- 1 red bell pepper cut into cubes
- ½ cup fresh or frozen peas
- 2½ cups paella rice such as Bomba
- 5 cups of hot chicken broth or mixture with clam juice
- 1 teaspoon smoked paprika
- 2 lemons cut into wedges (for serving)
- 2 tablespoons parsley chopped (for serving)

Directions

1. Season the chicken all over with salt and pepper.
2. In a paella pan or very large shallow skillet, pour in 2 tablespoons of olive oil over medium-high heat, and sear the chorizo until brown on all sides. Remove the chorizo, and set aside.

3. In the same pan, add chicken and brown it all over. Remove the chicken and set aside.
4. In the same pan, add the remaining two tablespoons of olive oil and onion. Sauté for 3-4 minutes. Add garlic and saffron threads. Sauté for 30 seconds.
5. Add ½ cup of wine and cook for 1 minute. Add the hand crushed tomatoes and the reserve tomato juice. Cook for 1 minute.
6. Add the chorizo, chicken and bay leaves. Bring this mixture to a boil.
7. Stir in the rice and half of the hot chicken broth. Cover it and simmer for 10 minutes under low heat checking frequently to see if more liquid is needed.
8. In a large pot, put clams and mussels over high heat with ½ cup of white wine. Cook for 10 minutes or until the shells are open. Discard the shells that do not open. Strain the liquid through a coffee filter or cheese cloth to remove sand. Add the strained liquid into the rice.
9. Stir the rice and add the calamari, shrimps, scallops, and peas. Check for liquid and seasoning. Add as needed. Cover the rice. Cook for 10 minutes more.
10. Add paprika to the rice mixture. Arrange the cooked mussels and clams by sticking them upright for the best appearance. Turn off heat. Cover it and let it stand covered before serving.

Tip

It is best to have all ingredients prepared before you start cooking.

Serving Suggestions

Top the dish with parsley, and serve hot. Arrange the lemon wedges on top of the paella.

Fish "en Papillote"

with Fennel Tapenade

Prep Time: 20 Min **Cook Time:** 20 Min **Total Time:** 40 Min

Serves 4

Fish prepared by wrapping food in a paper parcel rewards you by trapping all the delicious juices causing the fish to remain moist. When you cut into the bag, a cloud of aromatic steam erupts characterizing the succulent saturated flavors to follow.

Amount & Ingredients

Tapenade:

- 1 cup fennel fronds
- 2 tablespoons pitted Kalamata olives
- 2 tablespoons drained capers
- 2 anchovy filets
- 2 garlic cloves
- 2 tablespoons lemon juice
- 1 tablespoon lemon zest
- 2 tablespoons olive oil
- ½ teaspoon black pepper freshly ground

Fish "en Papillote":

- 2 tablespoons extra virgin olive oil
- 4 cups fennel bulbs thinly sliced
- 6 scallions thinly sliced
- 2 garlic cloves thinly sliced
- 1 teaspoon salt
- ½ teaspoon black pepper freshly ground
- ¼ cup lemon juice
- 1 tablespoon lemon zest
- 4 skinless red snapper (6 oz. pieces) or other firm white fish filets

Directions

To Prepare the Tapenade:

1. Preheat the oven to 400°F.
2. Cut off the fennel stalks and chop the fronds.
3. In a blender, combine the fennel, fronds, olives, capers, anchovies, garlic, lemon juice, zest, olive oil, salt and pepper. Pulse until chunky.

To Prepare the Fish "en Papillote":

1. In a large skillet over medium heat, add olive oil, fennel, scallions, and sauté for about 10 minutes.
2. Add garlic and sauté for 30 seconds more. Add salt, pepper, lemon juice and zest. Add 2 tablespoons of the prepared tapenade and mix thoroughly. Remove from heat.
3. Cut 4, 13-inch squares of parchment paper.
4. In the center of each parchment paper, put an equal portion of the fennel mixture.
5. Place one fish filet on top of each fennel mixture.

6. Sprinkle each filet with salt and pepper. Rub the top with 1 teaspoon of tapenade.
7. Fold the parchment paper over the fish tucking the ends under the fish to secure. Ensure the paper is well sealed otherwise steam will escape.
8. Arrange the parcel on a baking sheet and bake for 15-20 minutes depending on the fish thickness.

Tip

You can substitute a filet of halibut, salmon, trout or sole. Also, you can prepare this dish in advance by storing it in the refrigerator and baking it when needed.

Serving Suggestions

Cut open the parcel with scissors crosswise and promptly serve.

Marinated Sardines in a Blanket

on a Bed of Peppers and Onions

Prep Time: 15 Min **Cook Time:** 20 Min **Total Time:** 35 Min

Serves 4-5

This is a refreshing mezze on a hot evening especially while dining under the stars. They're high in Omega-3 with no mercury. Plus, they're easy to clean and prepare.

Amount & Ingredients

- 1 pound fresh sardines
- 1 jar grape leaves
- 2 tablespoons of olive oil
- 1 red bell pepper cut into thin strips
- 1 small red onion sliced thin
- 2 garlic cloves sliced thin
- 1 teaspoon oregano
- 2 teaspoons salt
- 1 teaspoon pepper
- 2 tablespoons parsley chopped
- 1 lemon cut into wedges

Directions

To prepare the fish:

1. Clean the sardines one at a time. Use a knife to remove scales, heads and innards. Leave the tails on.
2. Use the tip of a knife to loosen the spine and remove it from the body.
3. Rinse the fish thoroughly and put them in a colander to drain well.

To prepare the dish:

1. Preheat the oven to 450°F.
2. On a baking tray, spread the onions, pepper, garlic, oregano, salt, pepper and olive oil. Mix it well.
3. Put the baking tray into the preheated oven and bake for 10 minutes.
4. Meanwhile, spread the vine leaves on a flat surface.
5. Roll up each fish in a grape leaf, using 2 if needed, leaving the tail exposed. Brush each fish roll with olive oil.
6. Place the wrapped sardines on top of the pepper / onion mixture and bake 10 minutes more.

Tip

You can also make this fish on the outdoor grill. Using charcoal is best. Grill the fish over a hot fire for about 5 minutes per side. The grape leaves will protect the fish sealing in the juices.

Salmon Cakes

with Tantalizing Tartar Sauce

Prep Time: 15 Min **Cook Time:** 30 Min **Total Time:** 45 Min

Serves 2

If you love salmon, this is a tasty different way to consume your favorite fish. The cakes can be served with tartar celery root sauce.

Amount & Ingredients

- ½ pound salmon
- 2 tablespoons olive oil plus oil for frying
- ½ cup onion diced
- ½ cup celery diced
- ½ cup red bell pepper diced
- ¼ cup flat leaf parsley chopped
- 1 tablespoon capers drained and chopped
- 1 tablespoon Worcestershire sauce
- 1 teaspoon Old Bay seasoning
- 1 cup potatoes (about 2 small potatoes) boiled and mashed
- ½ cup light mayonnaise
- 1 tablespoon Dijon mustard
- 1 whole egg
- 1 egg white lightly beaten
- ¼ cup Panko bread crumbs &
- 1 cup Panko bread crumbs (for shaping salmon cakes)
- ½ cup cornmeal (for shaping salmon cakes)

Directions

1. Preheat the oven to 250°F.
2. Place the salmon on sheet pan. Brush with olive oil and sprinkle with salt (and pepper if desired). Roast for 15 minutes.
3. Remove the salmon from oven and let it cool.
4. Meanwhile, place 2 tablespoons of oil in a large sauté pan over medium heat. Add onion, celery and peppers. Sauté for 10 minutes.
5. Add Old Bay seasoning, Worcestershire sauce, capers and sauté for about 3 minutes.
6. Flake the salmon into a medium bowl. Add potatoes, mayonnaise, mustard, eggs, ¼ cup Panko and parsley.
7. Add the vegetable mixture to the salmon and combine it well.
8. Cover and chill in refrigerator for 30 minutes.
9. Shape into 8-10 round cakes. Dip them in the 1 cup Panko and cornmeal.
10. Heat 4 tablespoons of oil in a large pan over medium heat.
11. Add salmon cakes and fry 3-4 minutes each side. Keep them warm in the preheated oven.

Serving Suggestions

Serve on fresh kale or arugula leaves with tartar sauce.

Ocean Chosen

Sea Bass

with Fennel and Cherry Tomatoes

Prep Time: 10 Min **Cook Time:** 15 Min **Total Time:** 25 Min

Serves 4

A savory fish dish that's colorful, healthy and easy to prepare.

Amount & Ingredients

- 1 fennel bulb cut into thin slices
- 1 medium size red onion cut into thin slices
- 2 garlic cloves minced
- 2 cups multi-color cherry tomatoes
- 1 tablespoon chopped fresh thyme
- 1½ teaspoons black pepper freshly ground
- ½ teaspoon salt
- ⅓ cup pitted green olives sliced
- 2 tablespoons olive oil
- 1 pound skinned sea bass filet
- 2 tablespoons lemon juice
- ½ teaspoon salt
- ¼ teaspoon black pepper freshly ground
- ½ cup chopped basil leaves

Directions

1. Heat oven to 400°F.
2. In a large roasting pan, toss the fennel, onion, garlic, tomato, thyme, green olives, salt and pepper. Mix with 1 tablespoon of olive oil.
3. Roast the tomato mixture for 10 minutes.
4. In a large ovenproof skillet over high heat, add the remaining tablespoon of olive oil and swirl to coat.
5. Preheat the broiler to high.
6. Sprinkle the salt and pepper on the fish.
7. When the oil is hot, place the fish in the center of the skillet and sear one side for 2 minutes.
8. Drip lemon juice on top.
9. Put the skillet into the oven 6-7 inches from the broiler for 3 more minutes for medium rare and up to 8 minutes for well done.

Tip

Instead of sea bass you can use salmon or another fish of your liking.

Serving Suggestions

Place the fish on a serving plate and spoon the baked tomato and fennel on top and alongside of the fish. Sprinkle with chopped basil.

Shrimp
with Garlic and Ouzo

Prep Time: 15 Min | **Cook Time:** 10 Min | **Total Time:** 25 Min

Serves 4

An easy tasty dish that marries a traditional popular Greek alcohol with shrimp and garlic. It is especially gratifying when you have friends visiting your home.

Amount & Ingredients

- 12 deveined large shrimp with tails attached
- 1 tablespoon butter
- 1 tablespoon olive oil
- 1 teaspoon roughly cracked peppercorn
- ½ teaspoon salt
- 4 sliced garlic cloves
- ¼ cup ouzo
- 1 tablespoon chopped parsley
- 1 tablespoon finely chopped green onions

Garnish:

- 1 tablespoon chopped parsley
- 1 tablespoon finely chopped green onions

Directions

1. Rinse shrimp thoroughly and pat dry.
2. In a heavy bottom skillet (cast iron works well) over high heat, add butter and olive oil.
3. When the olive oil is hot and starts to smoke, add the shrimp, salt and pepper.
4. Sauté the shrimp for 2 minutes. Add garlic and sauté for 1 more minute.
5. Remove the skillet from heat.
6. Turn off heat and add ouzo.
7. Return the skillet to heat and simmer for 1 minute.

Tip

If you don't like the licorice taste of ouzo, you can substitute brandy.

Serving Suggestions

Serve the prawns hot with parsley and green onions on top. You may want to place the cast iron skillet in the middle of the table and let your guests serve themselves.

OUZO

Stuffed Calamari

with Vegetables and Marinara Sauce

Prep Time: 30 Min | Cook Time: 40 Min | Total Time: 1 Hr 10 Min

Serves 4

This flavorful dish was an appetizing tradition for my family and a favorite in my restaurants. It's tender, delectable and worth the effort.

Amount & Ingredients

Stuffing:

- 8 medium-sized whole squid, tubes cleaned
- 1 tablespoon olive oil
- ½ cup finely chopped green onions
- 2 garlic cloves minced
- 3 cups shredded green cabbage
- 1 cup peeled and shredded carrot
- 1 cup white mushrooms chopped into small cubes
- 1 cup red bell pepper chopped into small cubes
- 1 tablespoon fresh parsley
- ¼ cup toasted bread crumbs
- ¼ teaspoon black pepper freshly ground
- 1 teaspoon salt

Sauce:

- 1 tablespoon olive oil
- ½ cup white onion finely chopped
- 2 garlic cloves minced
- 1 teaspoon dry oregano
- 8 ounces canned small diced tomatoes
- 1 teaspoon basil finely chopped
- ½ teaspoon salt
- ¼ teaspoon black pepper freshly ground

Directions

To Prepare the Stuffing:

1. Preheat the oven to 375°F.
2. Clean the squid thoroughly and remove the heads from the tentacles. Discard heads.
3. Chop tender parts of tentacles into small pieces about ½-inch wide.
4. Heat olive oil in a large sauté pan over medium heat.
5. Add onion, garlic and chopped tentacles. Sauté for 2-3 minutes.
6. Add cabbage, carrots, mushrooms, red peppers, salt, pepper and parsley.
7. Sauté for 3-4 minutes.
8. Add bread crumbs and remove from heat.
9. Spoon the stuffing mixture loosely into each squid tube and close each with a tooth pick. Do not over stuff because the squid skin will shrink during cooking.

To Prepare the Marinara Sauce:

1. Heat oil over medium heat in a large ovenproof skillet that will hold squid in a single layer.
2. Add onion and garlic. Sauté for 2 minutes.
3. Add tomatoes, oregano, salt and pepper. Cook for 5 minutes.
4. Arrange the stuffed squid in the skillet with the tomato sauce.
5. Cover the skillet with an oven-proof lid or aluminum foil.
6. Bake for 30 minutes.
7. Remove foil and bake for 10 minutes more.
8. Remove from oven and sprinkle with fresh basil.

Tip

You can add some red pepper flakes in the stuffing to give a hint of heat.

Serving Suggestions

You can slice the squid and serve it with white rice or pasta.

Succulent Syros Seafood Rice

Prep Time: 20 Min **Cook Time:** 50 Min **Total Time:** 1 Hr 10 Min

Serves 6

Each bite from this dish delivers exotic flavors that will tantalize your palate. The recipe was created at my restaurant in Syros, Greece.

Amount & Ingredients

Sauce:

- 2 tablespoons olive oil
- 2 tablespoons butter
- 2 shallots finely chopped
- 2 garlic cloves minced
- ½ inch long fresh ginger finely chopped
- 1 tablespoon cardamom seeds
- 1 teaspoon turmeric
- 1 teaspoon saffron
- 4 tablespoons all-purpose flour
- 1 cup white wine
- 3-4 cups chicken stock
- ½ cup heavy cream
- 12 large deveined shrimp
- 12 black mussels scrubbed and washed
- ½ pound halibut cut into cubes
- 12 little neck clams scrubbed and washed

Rice:

- 2 tablespoons olive oil
- 1 tablespoon butter
- 2 garlic cloves minced
- 1 shallot finely chopped
- ½ inch long fresh ginger finely chopped
- 2 cups long grain rice
- 1 tablespoon cardamom seeds
- 1 teaspoon turmeric
- 1 teaspoon saffron
- 1 cup white wine
- 5 cups fish (or chicken) stock
- 1 teaspoon salt
- ¼ teaspoon black pepper freshly ground

Directions

To Prepare the Rice:

1. In a medium saucepan, heat oil and butter over medium heat.
2. Add ginger, shallots and garlic. Cook for 3-4 minutes.
3. Add rice and stir until rice is lightly toasted (about 1 minute).
4. Add cardamom seeds, turmeric, saffron and white wine. Stir and cook for 2 minutes.
5. Add stock, salt and pepper. Cover and cook for 20 minutes.
6. Cover saucepan with a kitchen towel. Keep it warm until serving.

To Prepare the Sauce:

1. Put the clams and a ½ cup of wine in a saucepan. Cook over medium-high heat for 2 minutes.
2. Add the mussels and cover for 3 more minutes until clams and mussels are open.

3. Remove and discard any clams or mussels that have not opened.
4. In a medium saucepan, put oil and butter over medium heat. Add shallots, garlic, ginger, cardamom seeds, turmeric and saffron.
5. Stir for 2 minutes, add flour and stir for another 2 minutes.
6. Strain the juice from the clams and mussels through a cheese cloth to eliminate sand.
7. Add the strained juice and ½ cup of wine to the flour mixture.
8. Stir in 2 cups of stock. If the sauce is too thick, add more stock.
9. Add shrimp and fish and cook for 5 minutes.
10. Add the prepared mussels, clams and heavy cream. Stir for 1-2 minutes.

Tip

You can use any kind of fish in place of the halibut such as salmon.

Serving Suggestions

Spoon rice into cylindrical mold or for a buffet use a tube cake mold. Turn mold over on serving plate. Remove the mold and spoon sauce on top of the rice. Surround the rice with seafood. Sprinkle with freshly cut parsley.

Chapter 6

Flap and Tap

A Poultry Party

A Parking Lot Too Far

Jake, a fifty-five-year-old athletic American writer and his middle-aged wife, Ariadni, an attractive Greek chef, travel through western Greece over a desolate country road in a dilapidated small borrowed Citroen.

JAKE
I'm hungry.

ARIADNI
Stop complaining. You ate 5 hours ago.
Maybe if you finished the breakfast I cooked
for you, -

JAKE
But, we've been looking -

A chicken darts across the road.

EERCEECH.

Jake slams on the brakes, barely missing the bird, which scurries through a parking lot of a less-than-welcoming Greek restaurant, Apolo's Arena.

JAKE
Damn chicken!

ARIADNI
Look, honey! We finally found a restaurant.

Spewing smoke, the car backfires...

BANG

... as it struggles to a parking spot.

Ariadni and Jake enter their culinary hole-in-the-wall to discover only one table has customers. It's occupied by four Greek farmers. Smoking, they exhale cumulus clouds of haze while drinking shots of Ouzo, a very popular Greek aperitif.

Ariadni motions Jake to an empty table that has a couple of menus on it. Their mouths water as they flip from one menu page to another.

A portly waiter in his late forties with a stained apron ambles towards the table.

ARIADNI
Wow! Look at this. They have Kremidopita,
stuffed grape leaves, grilled cala-

The waiter blurts,

WAITER
Forget the menu. We got one chicken in the oven. Take it or leave it?

Stunned, Jake gazes at his wife and quickly utters,

JAKE
We'll take it. With -

ARIADNI
A shot of Ouzo and a Coke Light.

Forty minutes later their waiter plops a platter with a smoldering whole chicken on the table, and...

JAKE
Hey, this chicken looks familiar.

ARIADNI
Looks like that parking lot was a bit too far for his own good.

...gives the Ouzo to Jake and the Coke to Ariadni.

Immediately, Ariadni switches the drinks and takes a sip of her Ouzo.

ARIADNI
Tasty.

Jake sips some Coke through a straw. The farm workers chuckle.

FIRST FARM WORKER
Americano.

SECOND FARM WORKER
Yeah, I hear Coke Light is a strong drink in America.

Laughing, they raise their shot glasses, chug their Ouzo and smile at the American novice spouting the Greek saying, "To your health,"

FARM WORKERS
Yasus!

ARIADNI
Yasus!

JAKE
Yasus!

JAKE
Honey, I can't wait for one of your meals.

ARIADNI
Hope you enjoy your Coke Light.

Cabbage Rolls

with Egg and Lemon Sauce

Prep Time: 45 Min   Cook Time: 1 Hr   Total Time: 1 Hr 45 Min

Serves 4-6

This nourishing meal is a definite crowd pleaser, especially during autumn when cabbages are freshly harvested. It's a delicious comfort food that's moist and savory. The lemony sauce provides a zesty taste that perfectly accents the turkey filling and cabbage.

Amount & Ingredients

Cabbage Rolls:

- 1 cup low sodium chicken stock
- 1 teaspoon salt
- 1 large head Napa cabbage
- 1 large onion sliced (for the bottom of the pan)

Stuffing:

- 1 pound ground turkey
- 2 onions finely chopped
- 4 scallions finely chopped
- ½ cup carrot grated
- ½ cup red bell pepper cut into small cubes
- ½ cup dill finely chopped
- ½ cup parsley finely chopped
- ½ cup arborio rice
- ¼ cup olive oil
- 1½ teaspoons salt
- ½ teaspoon black pepper freshly ground

Egg and Lemon Sauce:

- ½ cup fresh lemon juice
- 1 tablespoon lemon zest
- 2 egg yokes
- 2 teaspoons cornstarch diluted in 2 tablespoons of water
- ½ teaspoon salt
- ¼ teaspoon white pepper

Directions

To prepare the Cabbage Rolls:

1. Fill a large pot halfway with water and bring to a boil.
2. In the boiling water, cook the cabbage until the outside leaves fall off the head.
3. With tongs, remove soft leaves. Continue cooking until all leaves are soft and removed.
4. In a bowl, combine ground turkey, chopped onion, scallions, carrots, red pepper, dill, parsley, rice, olive oil, salt and pepper.
5. Place cabbage leaves on a work surface. Cut off any tough stems.
6. Place about 1 tablespoon of the turkey mixture on each cabbage leaf and roll each into a tight cylinder, being careful to fold the sides in just before finishing the cylinder.
7. Spread the sliced onion over the bottom of a large sauté pan.
8. Arrange the rolls in a row neatly over the onions seam-side down in a single layer.
9. Place a heavy plate on top of the cabbage rolls to weigh them down.

10. Cover the cabbage rolls with low sodium chicken stock or water. Add 1 teaspoon of salt and cover. Simmer over medium heat. Reduce heat to low and cook about 50 minutes.
11. Remove the pot from heat and carefully remove the plate.
12. Transfer the cabbage rolls to a deep serving platter reserving the cooking liquid.

To Prepare the Egg and Lemon sauce:

1. Pour the reserve cooking liquid into a small sauce pan over medium low heat. Add the diluted cornstarch and stir until the mixture slightly thickens.
2. Mix the eggs with lemon juice until foamy. Carefully pour this into the sauce pan stirring constantly for 1 minute. Add the lemon zest, ½ teaspoon salt and ¼ teaspoon white pepper. Remove from heat.
3. Spoon the sauce over the cabbage rolls.

Tip

You can substitute beef, pork or a mixture of both for the turkey.

Serving Suggestions

Put 4 cabbage rolls on each plate with the sauce on top. Serve with a colorful green salad. Also, the "Gotta Get It Biscuits" found in the Sides and Sandwiches (see page 167) chapter make a scrumptious addition.

Chicken with Okra

A Greek Version of a Latino Favorite

Prep Time: 15 Min **Cook Time:** 1 Hr **Total Time:** 1 Hr 15 Min

Serves 6

I went to a local supermarket and was surprised to find real Greek okra while looking for some ingredients to prepare a meal for my Latino friends. The wheels started turning. I thought why not combine the ingredients from a Latino dish with the Greek ones and surprise my guests with something new and exciting.

Amount & Ingredients

- 2 pounds okra
- 2 tablespoons red wine vinegar
- 2 teaspoons salt
- 1 skinned chicken cut into 8 pieces
- 4 tablespoons olive oil
- 1 jalapeño, seeds removed, and cut into small cubes
- 1 onion cut into small cubes
- 4 tomatillos cut into cubes
- 4 garlic cloves minced
- 1 teaspoon cumin
- ½ teaspoon cinnamon
- 1 teaspoon coriander
- 1 can (28 oz) diced tomatoes
- ½ teaspoon pepper

Directions

1. Preheat oven to 350°F.
2. Trim the stems from the okra and place them in a bowl. Add ½ teaspoon salt and vinegar. Toss to combine. Let this mixture sit for 30 minutes.
3. Meanwhile, season the chicken with salt and pepper.
4. In a large skillet, heat 2 tablespoons of olive oil and brown the chicken in batches. Set the chicken aside in a bowl.
5. In the same skillet, add the remaining 2 tablespoons of olive oil and onions. Sauté for 3-4 minutes. Add garlic and jalapeño. Cook for 2 minutes. Then add the tomatillo, cumin, cinnamon, coriander, diced tomatoes and the remaining 1 teaspoon of salt and pepper. Cook for 5 minutes.
6. Drain the okra and place it on a baking dish with the browned chicken.
7. Pour the tomato mixture on top of it, and cover with foil.
8. Place the dish in the preheated oven and cook for 45 minutes. Then, remove the foil and cook for 15 minutes more or until the chicken is brown and crispy.

Tip

You can fry some okra in olive oil and serve it on top of each dish.

Serving Suggestions

Serve over brown rice or polenta. Sprinkle chopped parsley and crumbled feta cheese over the top.

Flap & Tap

Cornish Hens

with Mustard Sauce

Prep Time: 20 Min **Cook Time:** 55 Min **Total Time:** 1 Hr 15 Min

Serves 4

These young tasty birds are a perfect serving size for one to two people and they cook faster than a full-grown chicken. The crispy top marries perfectly with the succulent juices captured by the potatoes.

Amount & Ingredients

Hens:

- 2 1-1¼ pound Cornish hens
- 1 teaspoon dry mustard
- ½ teaspoon water
- 6 tablespoons Dijon mustard
- 2 teaspoons salt
- 1 teaspoon freshly ground pepper
- 5 tablespoons extra virgin olive oil
- 1 cup Panko bread crumbs
- 1 medium onion peeled and diced
- 1 garlic clove finely chopped
- 1 teaspoon thyme
- 4 medium Yukon Gold potatoes peeled and sliced into ½ inch thick slices
- 2 tablespoons Italian parsley, finely chopped

Sauce:

- 2 tablespoons Dijon mustard
- 1 tablespoon ketchup
- 1 tablespoon steak sauce
- 1 teaspoon Worcestershire sauce
- 2 drops Tabasco sauce

Directions

To Prepare the Hens:

1. Preheat the oven to 400°F.
2. Dissolve the dry mustard in the water and then mix it into the Dijon mustard. Set it aside.
3. To remove the backbone, work on one hen at a time. Using scissors cut either side of the backbone and discard it. You can also ask your butcher to do this.
4. Lay the hens out flat, skin side up on a work surface. Using your hands press down on the breast bone of each hen to flatten it.
5. Season the Cornish hens on both sides with salt and pepper.
6. In a large sauté pan over medium heat, add two tablespoons oil. When the oil is hot, add the hens and cook 4-5 minutes on each side so that the birds become golden brown.
7. Remove birds from pan. Brush the skin sides with the mustard mixture and top with Panko, patting the crumbs into the mustard.

8. Wipe the pan, and over medium heat, add 3 tablespoons oil, onion, garlic, thyme and potatoes. Season with salt and pepper. Cook, stirring for about 8 minutes. Add chopped parsley to the potatoes.
9. Spread the potato mixture on a roasting pan and arrange the Cornish hens skin side up over the potatoes. Pour 2 tablespoons of oil over the hens and put in the preheated oven for 30 minutes or until they are cooked through.
10. Remove the hens from the oven and turn on the broiler.
11. Wrap the ends of the hens' legs with foil and put the hens under the broiler for 3-5 minutes until the mustard crumbs are brown and crisp.

To Prepare the Sauce

1. Whisk the mustard, ketchup, Worcestershire, steak sauce, and Tabasco to combine.

Tip

To get the best texture and taste, sear the butterflied hens first and then cook them through in the oven on a bed of potatoes. The potatoes will absorb all the cooking juices, creating a tasty dish.

Serving Suggestions

For each portion, place some potatoes on a serving plate and top with half a Cornish hen and enhance by drizzling the mustard sauce on top.

Creamy Chicken Crepes

Prep Time: 20 Min **Cook Time:** 1 Hr **Total Time:** 1 Hr 20 Min

Serves 6

The Greeks use and adapt many French recipes. This variation is very simple to make, yet delicious and sophisticated in flavor!

Amount & Ingredients

Crepes:

- 1 cup all-purpose flour
- 1 teaspoon salt
- ½ teaspoon white pepper
- 1 cup whole milk
- 4 large eggs

Chicken Filling:

- 2 pounds chicken breast with ribs
- 1 tablespoon olive oil
- 1 onion thinly sliced
- 1 celery stick thinly chopped
- 2 bay leaves
- 1 cup carrots thinly sliced
- 1 cup white wine
- 2 cups low sodium chicken stock
- 2 teaspoons salt
- 1 teaspoon black pepper freshly ground

White Sauce:

- 4 tablespoons butter
- 4 tablespoons flour
- ½ teaspoon salt
- ¼ teaspoon white pepper
- ½ cup grated Gruyère cheese
- 4 tablespoons grated Parmesan cheese

Directions

To Prepare the Crepes:

1. In a blender, combine all the crepe ingredients and process into a smooth batter. Cover and refrigerate for 1 hour.
2. Heat to medium-high a non-stick 6-8 inch skillet or a crepe pan.
3. When hot, spray the pan with olive oil.
4. Ladle about 2 ounces of the crepe batter into the skillet tilting the skillet to evenly coat the pan's surface with the batter.
5. Cook 1-2 minutes until the crepe's bottom is golden brown. With a spatula, turn the crepe and cook the other side about 40 seconds until slightly colored.
6. Transfer the crepe to a plate and cover. Repeat the process with the remaining batter.

To Prepare the Chicken Filling:

1. In a medium soup pot over medium-high heat, add olive oil, chicken and onion. Sauté for 5 minutes until chicken is seared on all sides.
2. Add celery, bay leaves, carrots, salt and pepper. Sauté for 5 minutes more.

3. Add wine. Simmer for 2-3 minutes. Add chicken stock. If needed, add some water to cover the chicken.
4. Simmer the chicken for about 40-45 minutes until the chicken is tender.
5. Remove the chicken from heat, strain it and reserve the vegetables. Discard the bay leaf.

To Prepare the White Sauce:

1. In a small sauce pan, melt the butter over medium heat.
2. Stir in the flour, salt and pepper until mixture is smooth.
3. Gradually add 2 cups of the reserve stock stirring constantly. Bring this to a boil. Cook for 2 minutes until thickened. If needed, add more stock.

To Prepare the Filling:

1. Preheat the oven to 350°F.
2. Remove the skin and bones from the chicken. Chop the chicken into small cubes.
3. In a medium bowl, combine the chicken with the reserve vegetables.
4. Pour some white sauce over the chicken, but reserve some for the topping.
5. Add the Gruyère and 2 tablespoons of Parmesan to the chicken mixture and combine.
6. Spread 2 tablespoons of the chicken mixture in the lower middle portion of each crepe and roll the crepe up. Place the crepe seam-side down in a greased baking dish. Repeat for the remaining crepes.
7. Drizzle the reserve white sauce over each crepe.
8. Sprinkle the remaining Parmesan cheese over the crepes.
9. Bake the crepes for 20 minutes or until they're bubbly.

Tip

You can add some sautéed spinach or asparagus as a variation. Also, you can make the crepes ahead of time, then refrigerate and bake later.

Serving Suggestions

Serve crepes warm with steamed vegetables and a green salad. They can be topped with fresh estragon(tarragon) for extra fragrance, flavor and color.

Oliga's Moroccan Chicken

Prep Time: 15 Min **Cook Time:** 40 Min **Total Time:** 55 Min

Serves 6

This exotic-tasting dish is thick with spices that will cause your taste buds to burst with pleasure, and its fragrant aromas make it a crowd favorite.

My Greek friend, Oliga, invited me to stay at her summer home in Skopelos, Greece, where she prepared this delightful meal and shared its wonderful recipe with me. We had a fantastic evening under the stars listening to great music while sipping shots of tsipouro, and enjoying her luscious dinner.

Amount & Ingredients

Chicken Stew:

- 1 whole organic chicken, skin removed, cut into pieces
- 2 teaspoons salt
- ½ teaspoon pepper
- ½ cup all-purpose flour
- ⅔ cup vegetable oil or mixed with olive oil
- 1 large onion chopped
- 2 large garlic cloves chopped
- 1 teaspoon turmeric
- 1 teaspoon ground cumin
- 1 teaspoon ground ginger
- ½ teaspoon paprika
- ½ teaspoon ground cinnamon
- 1 cinnamon stick
- 2 cups low sodium chicken broth
- 2 tablespoons honey
- ½ cup orange juice
- 2 tablespoons orange zest
- 2 tablespoons lime juice
- 1 cup pitted prunes
- 1 cup cooked chickpeas drained
- 2 tablespoons fresh cilantro chopped

Couscous:

- 1½ cups chicken broth
- 1 tablespoon olive oil
- 1 teaspoon saffron threads
- 3 tablespoons golden raisins
- 1 teaspoon salt
- 1½ cups whole grain couscous
- ½ cup flaked almonds toasted
- 1 tablespoon mint chopped (for serving)
- 1 tablespoon parsley chopped (for serving)

Directions

To Prepare the Stew:

1. Sprinkle chicken with 1 teaspoon of salt and pepper. Dust with flour shaking off any excess.
2. In a heavy-bottomed pot, add oil over medium-high heat. Brown the chicken 3-4 minutes each side, or until golden brown. Remove the chicken from the pot and set aside.

3. Put the onions in the same pot, and sauté for 3-5 minutes. Add garlic, turmeric, cumin, ginger and paprika, stirring for 1 minute.
4. Add the chicken broth, ground cinnamon, cinnamon stick, honey, orange juice, orange zest and lime juice to the pot.
5. Bring to a boil. Put the chicken back into the pot. Reduce the heat to low. Cover, and simmer for 20 minutes whisking occasionally.
6. Add the prunes, chickpeas, and simmer for 15 minutes more.
7. Check for seasoning. Keep the contents warm.

To Prepare the Couscous:

1. In a medium sauce pan, put the chicken broth, olive oil, saffron threads, raisins and salt. Bring to a boil.
2. Stir in couscous. Cover and remove from heat. Let stand for 5 minutes. Add almond flakes, mint, parsley, and fluff with a fork.

Tip

Vegetables and even meat can be changed according to taste, but squash, carrots, bell peppers, and lamb work well in this recipe.

Serving Suggestions

Serve chicken stew over couscous and top it with some toasted pine nuts or yogurt sauce (1 cup unsweetened Greek yogurt, 1 clove garlic minced, ½ teaspoon salt, ½ teaspoon paprika, ½ teaspoon cumin, 2-3 tablespoons of water). Mix to combine.

Orzo Casserole with Chicken

(Greek - *Yiouvetsi*)

Prep Time: 15 Min **Cook Time:** 1 Hr **Total Time:** 1 Hr 15 Min

Serves 4-5

This classic tasty dish is common throughout Greece. It's a comfort food that's relatively quick and simple to make.

Amount & Ingredients

- 3 tablespoons canola oil
- 1½ lbs. chicken skin off, cut into small portions
- 1 large red onion finely diced
- 2 teaspoons salt
- 2 garlic cloves minced
- ¼ cup white wine
- 1 10 ounce can diced tomatoes (preferably San Marzano)
- 1 red bell pepper cored, and cut into cubes
- 1 teaspoon Italian seasoning
- 1 teaspoon garam masala
- ½ teaspoon cumin
- ⅛ teaspoon crushed red pepper flakes
- 4 cups reduced sodium chicken broth
- 1½ cups orzo pasta
- ¼ cup grated Parmesan cheese
- 2 tablespoons parsley finely chopped

Directions

1. Preheat the oven to 350°F.
2. In a large sauté pan over medium-high heat, add oil.
3. Season the chicken with 1 teaspoon salt and brown in hot oil all over.
4. With a slotted spoon transfer the chicken to a large ovenproof dish.
5. Cover the chicken with foil and bake it for 30 minutes.
6. Meanwhile, in the same sauté pan, add the onion and sauté for 5 minutes.
7. Add garlic and sauté for 1 minute more.
8. Add wine, tomatoes, the remaining 1 teaspoon salt, peppers, pepper flakes, Italian seasoning, garam masala, cumin and chicken broth. Bring this mixture to a boil.
9. Add orzo and stir. Remove from heat.
10. Spread orzo mixture evenly around the chicken.
11. Place the baking pan back in the oven and bake mixture for 20 minutes more.
12. Stir occasionally. Add water or chicken broth if orzo seems too dry.
13. Check for seasoning.

Tip

Although the whole chicken (bone in) gives more flavors, this dish can be prepared using boneless chicken breasts. In Greece this dish is also made with lamb or beef. Seafood lovers can make this with shrimp.

Serving Suggestions

Arrange orzo mixture on a large ceramic platter. Sprinkle with Parmesan cheese and parsley. The dish can be served in 6" ramekins as shown above.

Stuffed Chicken Roulade

with Sun-Dried Tomatoes, Spinach and Feta

Prep Time: 30 Min　　Cook Time: 30 Min　　Total Time: 1 Hr

Serves 4

This fancy chicken pinwheel, filled with tender spinach, tangy feta and sweet sun-dried tomatoes, is an innovative way to break free from the usual chicken recipes but still leave your dinner guests completely satiated.

Amount & Ingredients

Chicken Breast:

- 4 boneless skin-on chicken breasts
- 4 tablespoons lemon juice
- 2 tablespoons lemon zest
- 1 teaspoon salt
- 1 teaspoon chopped rosemary
- 1 teaspoon dry oregano
- 1 teaspoon sage

Stuffing:

- 2 tablespoons olive oil
- ½ cup finely sliced green onions
- ½ cup leek thoroughly washed and finely sliced, white part only
- 6 ounces fresh baby spinach
- ¾ cup sun-dried tomato finely chopped
- 1 cup crumbled feta cheese
- ¼ cup bread crumbs
- ¼ cup Parmesan cheese
- 1 cup white wine

Directions

To Prepare the Chicken Breasts:

1. Put chicken breasts on top of a large piece of clear film (plastic wrap).
2. Cover breasts with another piece of clear film and pound the chicken to flatten.
3. Remove the top clear film and discard.
4. Drizzle lemon juice and lemon zest on the chicken.
5. Rub the chicken with rosemary, oregano and sage.
6. Season the chicken with salt and freshly ground pepper.

To Prepare the Stuffing:

1. In a medium skillet, heat the oil over medium heat.
2. Add onions and leeks, sautéing for 2-3 minutes.
3. Add spinach and sun-dried tomatoes and sauté 2-3 minutes more.
4. Remove mixture from heat and add feta, stirring gently.
5. Spread an equal amount of the spinach mixture on each chicken breast.

To Fold the Chicken:

1. Fold in the sides of each breast and roll up and secure with toothpicks.
2. If you wish, you can cover and refrigerate for 2-3 hours.

3. Preheat the oven to 400°F.
4. In an ovenproof dish, arrange the stuffed breasts in a single layer.
5. Season breasts with salt and pepper.
6. Mix bread crumbs and Parmesan cheese. Sprinkle this over the chicken breasts.
7. Cover the pan with aluminum foil.
8. Bake for 15 minutes.
9. Remove foil. Add white wine and bake another 15 minutes.
10. Remove chicken from the pan and place it on a serving plate.
11. Cover with foil or a large lid to keep warm.

To Prepare the Gravy:

1. Mix 1 tablespoon of cornstarch with 2 tablespoons of water in a small mixing bowl.
2. In a small saucepan over medium heat, strain the juice from the cooking pan.
3. Deglaze (see page 209) the cooking pan with a little water, emptying the contents into the saucepan.
4. Bring the saucepan to a boil for 3 minutes.
5. Add the cornstarch mixture, stirring until the sauce thickens.

Tip

If your butcher can debone and butterfly a chicken, you can use the whole bird. Put the stuffing in. Roll up the bird and secure with a cooking string.

Serving Suggestions

Pour half the gravy on top of the chicken breasts. Pour the remaining gravy into a serving bowl. Serve chicken with Stefania's Roasted Potatoes (see page 175).

Chapter 7

Marvelous Meats

Grandma Always Knows Best

The afternoon sun radiates off a variety of bronze pots and graters dangling from the walls of a Greek kitchen in Syros, Greece. Homemade sauces and jams proliferate the open cupboards. This culinary paradise can cultivate a young child's desire to become a world-class chef.

Stefania, an attractive hyper-active twelve-year-old child, intently assists her grandmother, Sophia, who's preparing a meal using a wood-burning stove. Her recipe is a family secret and each grandchild realizes it is an honor to be given the ingredients and directions.

STEFANIA
Please Granny, you promised last year!

Granny gives Stefania a stern look.

SOPHIA
It's going to be a while before I take a chance trusting you with my famous beef roll recipe.

STEFANIA
Let me try. It's Eirini's name day. I want to surprise her.

Stefania yanks on Sophia's apron.

STEFANIA
Come on, Grandma, I want to be a great chef... like you.

A look of opportunity overcomes Granny's face as she seizes the chance to mold her grandchild's life. She expounds sternly,

SOPHIA
On one condition: you must follow my recipe directions explicitly.

Stefania nods that she understands declaring,

STEFANIA
I promise. I promise, Grandma.

SOPHIA
Bravo! I can go for my afternoon walk relaxed while you take care of the beef rolls.

Granny struts across the kitchen to a small antique iron safe, unlocks it, and carefully selects her prize recipe. It appears to be written on parchment paper. Stefania's eyes widen as Granny turns and approaches her.

SOPHIA
Here it is Stefania. I'm counting on you.

As Sophia hands Stefania the recipe, the sun illuminates the recipe. A flash of light signifies the transfer of trust from one generation to another.

Sophia slips out the back door as Stefania goes to work intensely chopping parsley, basil and garlic. She quickly pounds the beef to tenderize it, dancing around the preparation table, tossing a pinch of salt and pepper on the meat as if she were a master chef.

Yannis, Stefania's older brother, who's sixteen pops in the back door. He's clever and devious.

YANNIS
What's cook'n?

He inspects the ingredients on the table.

YANNIS
Wow, Granny's famous beef rolls.

STEFANIA
Yes. It's my big chance to prove I can prepare a great meal by myself.

YANIS
You're joking? You're cooking it by yourself?

STEFANIA
Don't bug me. I've got things under control.

Yannis carefully inspects the meat.

YANNIS
Of course you do. But, it looks like you forgot the two tablespoons of red pepper flakes.

STEFANIA
That's not in the recipe!

YANNIS
Sure it is. Granny's getting old. She forgot to write it down.

STEFANIA
Yannis, you're not going to fool me.

YANNIS
Remember the last time you didn't listen to me? You got into big trouble.

Stefania tilts her head to one side questioning Yannis but adds the flakes.

Soon the afternoon fades into evening. The stars come out as a gentle breeze signifies the start of a perfect Greek evening. Happiness and love permeate the air.

Two dozen hungry guests pack the dining room table devouring Granny's appetizers anxiously waiting for the star attraction, the beef rolls. The guests dip mustard batons (see page 39) and Syros squash blossoms (see page 53) into edamame hummus (see page 37) and olive pâté (see page 47). Their anticipation rises.

HUNGRY GUEST 1
Hey Granny, where's your famous beef rolls?

SOPHIA
Try some stuffed tomatoes (see page 57).
Stefania's prepared the rolls.

HUNGRY GUEST 2
What? Yannis' baby sister? What the heck
does she know about cooking?

STEFANIA
Hold your donkeys. They'll be out in a second,
and be just as tasty as Granny's.

A few guests chuckle.

Stefania prances to the oven but turns and gives the guests a grin of complete confidence.

She flings open the oven door and retrieves a tray of sizzling beef rolls. The guests lift their noses high and begin inhaling the wonderful aroma of the rolls.

As Stefania places a platter of beef rolls on the dining table, a feeding frenzy erupts among the guests, each trying to be the first to grab a roll.

The guests quickly stuff their faces. Immediately, however, their eyes water. Perspiration pours from their faces and steam erupts from their noses.

HUNGRY GUEST 1
Mamma Mia! That's a spicy beef roll!

HUNGRY GUEST 2
Where's the fire hose?

HUNGRY GUEST 3
Holy lightning bolts of Zeus! What the Hell's in
this? A matchbox?

HUNGRY GUEST 4
Mt. Vesuvius!

A look of shock overcomes Stefania. She whips around glaring at Yannis in the corner who's doubled over laughing.

STEFANIA
Yannis, you jerk. You ruined my meal. I'll never
be a chef.

Sophia rushes to Stefania and...

SOPHIA
It's OK honey.

...gives Stefania a big hug.

SOPHIA
We all have to learn to follow directions.
You're a lot smarter chef now... Someday
you'll be known world-wide.

Stefania, with tears in her eyes, kisses Sophia on the cheek.

STEFANIA
Granny, you always know best.

See recipe on page 131.

Beef Stew

with Prunes and Dark Beer

Prep Time: 20 Min **Cook Time:** 1 Hr 45 Min **Total Time:** 2 Hr 5 Min

Serves 6

When dining with family or friends on a cold night, a large pot of tasty hearty stew is a welcome sight, especially when it's enriched with dark beer or ale.

Amount & Ingredients

- ½ cup all-purpose flour
- 2 pounds boneless beef chuck / pot roast, cut into cubes
- 3 tablespoons olive oil
- 1½ cups chopped onions
- 1 12 ounce bottle of Guinness stout
- 1 cup turnips peeled and cut into cubes
- 1½ cups beef or chicken broth
- 1½ cups carrots peeled and cut into chunks
- 1 cup pitted prunes
- 1 teaspoon salt
- ½ teaspoon black pepper freshly ground
- 2 tablespoons chopped parsley

Directions

1. In a large saucepan or Dutch oven, heat the olive oil over medium heat.
2. Dust the beef with flour and brown a few at a time in the oil.
3. Remove beef and place on a plate.
4. In the same saucepan, add onions and sauté for 5 minutes.
5. Add beer and broth. Bring the mixture to a boil.
6. Return the beef to the saucepan.
7. Add turnip and carrot pieces. Cover and simmer over low heat for about 1½ hours.
8. Add the prunes, salt and pepper. Cook 15 minutes more or until beef is fork tender.
9. Check for seasoning.
10. Serve hot with fresh parsley sprinkled on top.

Serving Suggestions

You can serve with potato salad or Stefania's Roasted Potatoes (see page 175).

Granny's Beef Rolls

Prep Time: 15 Min **Cook Time:** 1 Hr 45 Min **Total Time:** 2 Hrs

Serves 6

This recipe came from my grandmother who made it on special occasions such as "Name Days" and birthdays. In Greece, everyone's name has a special celebration date called a "Name Day," which is celebrated as enthusiastically as birthdays.

During my childhood, my sisters, brother and I always looked forward to having this divine dish that left us licking our lips.

Amount & Ingredients

- 1½ pounds beef round steaks thinly sliced
- 1 teaspoon salt
- ½ teaspoon black pepper freshly ground
- 1 cup dry bread crumbs
- 4 garlic cloves minced
- ½ cup finely chopped parsley
- 1 tablespoon finely chopped basil
- 2 tablespoons olive oil
- 4 cups marinara sauce

Directions

1. Pound meat to flatten and tenderize.
2. Sprinkle with salt and pepper.
3. Cut the meat into 4-6 inch squares.
4. Combine bread crumbs, garlic, parsley and basil.
5. Place a heaping tablespoon of crumb mixture onto each meat square and roll up the beef.
6. Secure the meat with a cooking string or toothpick.
7. In a large skillet, add the olive oil over medium-high heat and brown beef rolls on all sides.
8. Pour marinara sauce in a large saucepan over medium heat and bring it to a boil.
9. Add the beef rolls. Lower the heat to low and simmer for about 1-1½ hours until beef rolls are tender.
10. If the sauce is too thick, add some water.

Tip

Instead of cutting beef into squares, you can use the whole piece which will make a long roll.

Serving Suggestions

Slice the beef roll into 1-inch wide pieces. Serve hot over pasta or mashed potatoes.

Greek Veal

with Quinces

Prep Time: 20 Min   Cook Time: 1 Hr 45 Min   Total Time: 2 Hr 5 Min

Serves 6

This was my father's favorite dish. The yellow quince fruit is generally available in the fall. At this time, they have a very aromatic smell and add a special touch to your creation. Their tangy taste creates a synergetic combination with the veal.

Amount & Ingredients

- 2½ pounds lean boneless veal shoulder, cut into 1½-inch cubes
- ½ cup all-purpose flour
- 4 tablespoons olive oil
- ½ cup red onion finely chopped
- 2 garlic cloves minced
- 1 cup red wine
- 1 tablespoon tomato paste
- 1 cinnamon stick
- 2 whole bay leaves
- 1 teaspoon salt
- ½ teaspoon black pepper freshly ground
- 3 medium quinces peeled, cored and cut into thick wedges
- 2 tablespoons honey
- 20 whole white frozen pearl onions
- ½ teaspoon sweet paprika
- 1 tablespoon lemon juice
- 2 tablespoons chopped fresh parsley

Directions

1. Heat 2 tablespoons of olive oil in a large heavy-bottomed saucepan over medium-high heat.
2. Dust the veal pieces with flour and brown a few at a time in olive oil.
3. Place the veal on a platter.
4. In the same saucepan over medium heat, add the chopped onions and sauté for 3-4 minutes.
5. Add garlic and sauté for 30 seconds.
6. Add the wine and stock. Bring the mixture to a boil.
7. Return veal to the saucepan along with the tomato paste, cinnamon stick, bay leaves, salt and pepper.
8. Reduce heat to low. Cover and simmer for about 1 hour.
9. Next, in a large skillet over medium heat, add the remaining 2 tablespoons of olive oil.
10. Add quince and pearl onions. Sauté, stirring occasionally for 4-5 minutes.
11. Add honey and ½ cup of water to quince. Simmer until they are soft and light golden (about 20 minutes).

12. In the saucepan with the veal, stir in the quinces and pearl onions adding the lemon juice and paprika.
13. Taste for salt and pepper.
14. Simmer over low heat for another 30 minutes until meat is tender.
15. Remove the cinnamon stick and bay leaves.
16. Serve hot.
17. Sprinkle with parsley.

Serving Suggestions

Serve with Stefania's Roasted Potatoes (see page 175).

Lamb

with Spinach and Dried Apricots

Prep Time: 10 Min **Cook Time:** 2 Hr **Total Time:** 2 Hr 10 Min

Serves 6

This delicious Mediterranean stew gets numerous exotic flavors from dried fruits as well as a spicy hint from ginger and cinnamon.

Amount & Ingredients

- 2 tablespoons olive oil
- 1½ pound boneless lamb stew meat
- ½ cup all-purpose flour
- 1 cup chopped white and green scallions
- 2 garlic cloves minced
- 1 fresh ginger root peeled and chopped thinly
- ¼ teaspoon ground cinnamon
- ¾ cup dried pitted apricot
- 1½ pound fresh spinach washed and roughly chopped
- ⅓ cup fresh chopped dill
- 1 cup white wine

Garnish:

- ¼ cup sliced roasted almonds

Directions

1. Over medium-high heat in a large heavy pot, heat 1 tablespoon olive oil.
2. Season lamb with salt and pepper. Dust with flour.
3. Brown lamb pieces a few at a time in the hot oil and transfer to a plate.
4. In the same pot, add 1 tablespoon olive oil. Over medium heat, add onions, ginger, garlic and cinnamon.
5. Sauté for 2-3 minutes.
6. Add the wine and return the lamb to the pot. Simmer for about 30 minutes.
7. If there is not enough liquid, add some hot water.
8. Rinse the apricots and put them into the pot with the lamb.
9. Cover and cook 15-20 minutes more or until lamb is tender.
10. Add the washed spinach to the lamb. Push down the spinach to incorporate with the rest of the ingredients.
11. Add the dill and cook for 5 minutes more.

Tip

If the sauce is watery, dilute 2 tablespoons of cornstarch with 1 tablespoon of water and stir this into the sauce to thicken.

Serving Suggestions

You can serve this dish with rice or couscous. Also, roasted almonds can be sprinkled on top for extra flavor.

Seared Pork Chops

with Honey and Pomegranate Seeds

Prep Time: 15 Min **Cook Time:** 15 Min **Total Time:** 30 Min

Serves 4

This robust meal features succulent pork chops. The marinade gives a tantalizing flavor while also tenderizing the meat.

Amount & Ingredients

- 4 bone-in pork chops, 8-ounces each and ¾-inch thick
- 2 tablespoons soy sauce
- 2 tablespoons minced garlic
- 1 tablespoon rice vinegar
- 2 tablespoons grated ginger
- 2 tablespoons olive oil
- 2 tablespoons honey
- 1 cup pomegranate juice
- 1 teaspoon dissolved cornstarch in 2 tablespoons of water
- ¼ cup pomegranate seeds

Directions

To Prepare the Marinade:

1. Place pork chops in a large closeable food storage bag. Pour soy sauce, garlic, rice vinegar and ginger over the pork chops and close the bag.
2. Flip the chops once halfway through the 30-45 minute marinating process.

To Prepare (Sear) the Pork Chop:

1. Heat the olive oil in a large skillet over medium-high heat.
2. Remove pork chops from the marinade and sear for about 4 minutes on each side.
3. Reduce heat to medium-low and flip chops and cook 4 minutes more or until just cooked through.
4. Move pork chops to a platter and let rest for 10 minutes.

To Prepare the Sauce:

1. In the same skillet, add honey, pomegranate juice, the remaining marinade and cornstarch. Simmer over medium heat until the mixture thickens.
2. Spoon the sauce over the pork chops and garnish with pomegranates seeds.

Tip

If the sauce is too thin, dilute 1 tablespoon of cornstarch with 2 tablespoons of water and mix it into the sauce.

Serving Suggestions

Slice the pork chops and drizzle the pomegranate sauce over them. Serve with rice or potatoes.

Chapter 8

Vibrant Vegetables

A Kale of Two Ladies

Today the earth is cherished, especially in Syros, Greece. It's "Earth Day" and a well-known coastal villa is completely booked with foreign guests on this toasty summer afternoon. In the distance a few menacing clouds coagulate.

However, as the guests foster a festive mood inside the villa, Eirini reminds her sister, Stefania, the villa's Greek chef, the importance of our environment.

EIRINI
We must be kind to the earth. Respect our habitat.

STEFANIA
Yes. We should do something today to teach the guests' children how important it is to care for our planet and what nature provides us with.

A crowd of six adult male guests gather in the villa's rustic sitting room. Antique furniture, a fireplace, and classic books embellish the area.

A corpulent guest, Nick, the leader of group, rubs his belly.

NICK
Don't worry fellas. I'll make sure you have some home-cooked chow that'll really fill your bellies.

Nick pops into the villa's kitchen.

NICK
Excuse me, chef. We're taking the speedboat out. We'd like some ribs, fries, coleslaw and biscuits with gravy for dinner. Can you handle that?

STEFANIA
Sure, but I can also prepare a salad rich in vitamins C, B12 and A accompanied by seafood and vibrant vegetables.

NICK
(sternly)
Forget that sissy stuff. Just have the ribs ready.

Nick turns abruptly, and rushes through the kitchen's door.

Shortly, the guests depart the villa's dock in their rented speedboat for the bay off Kini Beach. They've hired a Greek musician, Georios, to play guitar and sing Greek music. Their party ignites immediately as they begin consuming Mythos beer. Three or four guests remain standing as the boat arrives at their destination.

NICK
Hey, give Luke a beer.

A guest tosses Luke a can of beer. However, drinking heavily the guests don't notice the surf intensifying.

A lightning bolt strikes the sea three miles away.

BOOM!

A medium size wave slams the side of the boat jarring the occupants.

NICK
Holy Toledo! Luke, quick, drop the anchor!

Spontaneously, Luke turns around, grabs the fifty-pound anchor that's on the deck, and shoves it off the port side of the boat.

CA-PLUNK.

But, there's one small problem: he didn't attach a rope or chain to the anchor.

LUKE
Oh-

NICK
Nice going, "Cool Hand."

LUKE
What'll we do now? We're drifting out to sea!

NICK
Keep cool, "Cool Hand." I'll just start the engine and we'll pull the dang boat up on shore and continue the party.

Nick turns the ignition key.

SPUTTER.

He tries again.

SPUTTER. The engine expels its last breath. HISS and grinds to a halt.

Stefania and Eirini are in the villa's kitchen preparing dinner. The old-fashioned house phone rings. Stefania nonchalantly answers.

NICK
(panicky)
Stefania is that you? You gotta get out here right away. We lost the anchor, and the freak'n motor won't start, and-

STEFANIA
Relax. Don't have a heart attack before your rib dinner. We'll be there in a few minutes.

NICK
Hurry! Forget the ribs. Just get over here with a tow boat right away. We'll eat that healthy salad, and-

STEFANIA
Nick, take it easy. We're coming.

Stefania and Eirini stroll out the kitchen door.

STEFANIA
(calmly)
Yep, somebody's done it again this year.

EIRINI
Grab your scuba gear. I'll get the car.

A minute later Stefania piles her scuba gear into an archaic small Toyota and the girls depart for Kini Beach. When they arrive, they spot the helpless speedboat only three hundred feet offshore with the occupants frantically yelling and waving at them for help.

Stefania grins at the guests and slowly dons her scuba gear.

EIRINI
(taking her time)
While you're out there, get something for "Earth Day" dinner like kelp or seaweed. You might as well pick up some sea urchins and mussels.

STEFANIA
You know me. I'm going to have some fun out there.

The sisters chuckle.

Stefania leisurely swims out to the boat, winks at Nick and dives. While gathering fresh seaweed, she captures a dozen sea urchins and mussels. A few minutes later, she attaches a rope to the anchor and yanks on the rope signifying it's finally time to haul in the anchor.

Shortly, the girls prepare for a different type of dinner party. This one features a kale and seaweed salad, seaweed pasta with mussels and sea urchins to honor the natural bounty of the earth.

The guests, including Nick with his six and eight-year-old daughters, sit at a long polished wooden dining room table. Large open doors provide a picturesque view of the storm clouds over the Aegean Sea.

With sparks in their steps Stefania and Eirini approach Nick's family carrying their "Earth Day" culinary creations.

STEFANIA
Nick, try this. You might like it.

NICK
Ah -

She serves Nick a kale seaweed salad with sesame and ginger. Nick cautiously takes a bite.

NICK
Yum. This is tasty!

EIRINI
Try the pasta.

STEFANIA
The sea urchins too.

Nick's daughters spontaneously serve themselves to the "Earth Day" harvest.

They take a few bites and gaze at their father.

AMY
This is good daddy.

TAMI
Can we eat like this every day when we get back to Texas?

A shocked Nick gazes at Stefania.

NICK
(whimpering)
What have you gotten me into?

Acorn Squash

Stuffed with Mushroom Risotto

Prep Time: 15 Min **Cook Time:** 50 Min **Total Time:** 1 Hr 5 Min

Serves 4

This flavorsome dish is an excellent choice as a nourishing entrée for a quiet evening at home.

Amount & Ingredients

- 2 tablespoons olive oil
- 1 cup chopped onion
- 1 tablespoon fresh thyme leaves
- 1 cup sliced mushrooms
- 1 cup arborio rice
- ½ cup white wine
- 3 cups low sodium veggie stock
- 1 cup butternut squash – peeled, deseeded and cut into small cubes
- 2 acorn or carnival squash
- 2 tablespoons chopped parsley
- ⅔ cup Parmesan (or crumbled feta cheese - optional)

Directions

1. Preheat the oven to 350°F.
2. Pierce each squash with a knife in several places.
3. Microwave the squashes on high 12-14 minutes or until tender turning upside down once. Let them stand for 5 minutes.
4. Cut each squash in half length-wise. Scoop out seeds.
5. Arrange squash halves cut side up on a baking sheet.
6. Heat the oil in a large sauce pan. Sauté the onion until softened but not colored.
7. Add the mushrooms to the sauté pan and cook about 2 minutes.
8. Add the rice to the pan and stir continuously for 3 minutes.
9. Add the wine and cook for another 3 minutes to evaporate the alcohol.
10. Add the butternut squash cubes and stir for 2 minutes.
11. Start to add the warm stock a little at a time, stirring occasionally. Allow the rice to absorb the liquid before adding more.
12. Season the mixture and cook gently for about 20 minutes. When most of the liquid has been absorbed, remove from heat.
13. Optional: If you wish to include feta cheese, sprinkle it on top now.
14. Spoon the risotto into the baked squash. Sprinkle with parsley. Cover with foil and bake for 15 minutes.

Tip

Other types of squashes such as calabaza squash, kabocha squash or spaghetti squash may be used.

Serving Suggestions

Serve warm immediately and dust with Parmesan cheese.

Artichoke – "à la Polita"

Prep Time: 30 Min | Cook Time: 30 Min | Total Time: 1 Hr

Serves 6-8

This lemony Greek artichoke stew is not only delicious but it's also a super scrumptious vegan dish. Using fresh artichokes is a tedious job but the effort is worth it.

Amount & Ingredients

- 10 fresh artichokes
- 1 lemon
- 2 tablespoons olive oil
- 10 pearl onions
- 6 green onions thinly sliced
- 1½ cups fava beans popped out of their skin
- 1½ cups sweet peas
- 1 cup carrots thinly sliced
- 1 cup vegetable broth
- 1 teaspoon salt
- ½ teaspoon black pepper freshly ground
- 1 tablespoon chopped parsley
- 1 tablespoon chopped dill
- ⅓ cup lemon juice
- 1 tablespoon cornstarch

Directions

1. Working with one artichoke at a time, remove and discard the tough outer leaves.
2. Remove the hair choke from the center and place the artichoke in a bowl filled with cold water, salt and lemon slices.
3. In a sauté pan over medium heat, add olive oil, pearl onions and green onions.
4. Sauté for 10 minutes.
5. Add the artichokes, fava beans, peas, carrots, broth, salt and pepper.
6. Simmer for 25 minutes.
7. Add the dill and parsley, leaving some for serving.
8. In a small bowl, mix the cornstarch and lemon juice. Pour this into the artichoke mixture stirring gently to thicken the pan's liquid and cook for an additional 5 minutes.

Tip

You can use frozen artichoke hearts, fava beans and peas if needed.

Serving Suggestions

Arrange the artichoke mixture attractively on a serving platter. You may serve this as either a main or side dish on fresh parsley and dill on top.

Artichokes

with Tomatoes and Soya Beans

Prep Time: 1 Hr **Cook Time:** 25 Min **Total Time:** 1 Hr 25 Min

Serves 4

This soup is a refreshing dish on a hot evening while dining under the stars.

Amount & Ingredients

- 8 fresh artichokes
- 2 lemons cut in half
- 1 tablespoon olive oil
- 1 cup whole pearl onions peeled
- ½ cup green onion sliced
- 1 cup fennel sliced
- 1 cup carrots sliced
- 1 cup soya beans shelled
- 1 cup potatoes peeled and cut into small cubes
- 2 cups tomatoes skinned and chopped into small cubes
- ½ cup sun-dried tomatoes julienned cut
- 1 cup hot water if needed
- 2 tablespoons parsley roughly chopped

Directions

1. Working with one artichoke at a time, remove and discard the tough outer leaves.
2. Remove the hair choke from the center and place the artichoke in a bowl filled with cold water, salt and lemon slices.
3. In a sauté pan over medium heat, add olive oil, pearl onions and green onions. Sauté for 10 minutes.
4. Add to the pan the prepared artichokes, fennel, carrots, potatoes and tomatoes. Simmer for 10 minutes. Check liquid level, and add hot water if needed.
5. Add soya beans, and simmer for 4-5 minutes.
6. Check for seasoning and add if needed.

Tip

If needed, you can use frozen artichokes hearts.

Serving Suggestions

Arrange the artichokes on a platter and surround them with onions and soya beans. Sprinkle with parsley.

Braised Escarole

with Black-eyed Beans

Prep Time: 15 Min | Cook Time: 40-55 Min | Total Time: 55-70 Min

Serves 4-6

A healthy, nutritious, filling dish that works well accompanying meat and fish.

Amount & Ingredients

- 1½ cups dried black-eyed beans
- 1 head escarole chopped and washed thoroughly
- 2 tablespoons olive oil
- 2 shallots thinly sliced
- 2 garlic cloves minced
- 1 teaspoon lemon zest
- 1 red bell pepper cut into small cubes
- 2 tablespoons lemon juice
- 1 teaspoon cornstarch
- 1 teaspoon salt
- ½ teaspoon pepper

Directions

1. Soak the beans for 3-4 hours or overnight.
2. Drain the beans and place them in a sauce pan. Cover with water and boil over low heat for 30-45 minutes until tender but not mushy. Then drain the beans again.
3. In a large sauce pan over medium heat, add olive oil and shallots. Sauté for 3-4 minutes. Add the garlic and sauté for 1 more minute.
4. Add escarole and red pepper. Sauté for 5 minutes.
5. Add the beans and simmer for 10 minutes.
6. In a small bowl, mix the cornstarch, lemon juice and lemon zest.
7. Mix this into the escarole mixture so it will thicken the sauce. If needed, add 1 tablespoon of water.
8. Add salt and pepper to taste.

Tip

Instead of escarole you can substitute spinach, Swiss chard, kale or a combination of these greens.

Serving Suggestions

This dish can be served as an entrée or vegetarian dish with rice.

Eggplant Soufflé Delagraciano

Prep Time: 40 Min | Cook Time: 1 Hr | Total Time: 1 Hr 40 Min

Serves 6

This dish takes its name from a village on the Greek island of Syros. It's a rich meal whose cheese, tomato and eggplant ingredients deliver a synergistic flavor combination.

Amount & Ingredients

Eggplant:

- 4-5 eggplants skinned and cut into thin slices
- 2 tablespoons salt
- ½ cup olive oil

Sauce:

- ⅓ cup olive oil
- 1 cup onion, diced small
- 4 minced garlic cloves
- 3 cups canned small diced tomatoes with juice
- 1 tablespoon mirin
- 1 teaspoon crushed red pepper flakes
- 1 teaspoon dried oregano
- ½ cup toasted bread crumbs
- 3 cups grated Gruyere or Italian Fontina cheese
- 1 cup grated Parmesan (Parmigiano-Reggiano) cheese

Topping:

- 2 cups fat-free sour cream
- 5 eggs
- 2 tablespoons grated Parmesan
- 2 tablespoons toasted bread crumbs
- 1 teaspoon pepper

Directions

To Prepare the Eggplant:

1. Generously salt the eggplant slices and let them drain through the colander for 1 hour.
2. Rinse the eggplant slices thoroughly and pat dry with a paper towel.
3. Preheat the oven to 400°F.
4. Prepare a large baking sheet by spreading olive oil generously over its surface.
5. Spread the eggplant in a single layer on the baking sheet brushing olive oil liberally on top.
6. Bake the eggplant for approximately 20 minutes until it is tender and golden. Repeat this process until all the eggplant is used.

To Prepare the Sauce:

1. In a large skillet over medium temperature, heat the olive oil, and sauté the onions for 5 minutes or until the onion is soft.
2. Add the garlic and sauté for 1 more minute.
3. Add the tomatoes, mirin, pepper flakes and oregano. Reduce the heat to low, and simmer about 30 minutes until sauce has thickened.

To Prepare the Dish:

1. Lightly coat 6 (8-ounce each) soufflé dishes with cooking spray.
2. Sprinkle the bottom with bread crumbs.
3. Mix the 2 cheeses spreading half of the mixed cheese equally among the 6 soufflé dishes.
4. Layer half of the cooked eggplant slices over the cheese.
5. Pour the tomato sauce over the eggplant slices and scatter ¼ of the leftover cheese on top.
6. Repeat the above to make another layer.
7. Scatter the remaining cheese mixture on top.

To Prepare the Topping:

1. Preheat the oven to 350°F.
2. In a medium bowl, whisk together sour cream, eggs and pepper (to taste).
3. Pour slowly an equal amount of the egg mixture over the soufflé dishes.
4. Make several incisions with a knife all the way through the eggplant, and let it stand 30 minutes to allow the custard to soak into the soufflé.
5. Mix the Parmesan and bread crumbs. Sprinkle over the top of the soufflé dishes.
6. Bake the soufflé in the lower part of the oven for 30 minutes until golden and puffy.

Tip

You can, if you desire, prepare the dish the day before up to the point where you place the topping.

Serving Suggestions

You can serve this dish as a starter, or as an entrée with a colorful green salad.

Rockin' Ratatouille

(Greek - *Briám* or *Tourloú*)

Prep Time: 20 Min | Cook Time: 55 Min | Total Time: 1 Hr 15 Min

Serves 6

Ratatouille originated in the area around present day Occitan Provença, France, but is a common Greek dish called *briám* or *tourloú*. It's usually served as a side dish but may also be served as a full meal. It's a true taste of summer.

Amount & Ingredients

- ½ cup olive oil
- 1 medium eggplant cut into ½-inch cubes
- 1 large zucchini cut into ½-inch cubes
- 1 large yellow squash cut into ½-inch cubes
- 1 red bell pepper, seeds and stem removed, cut into ½-inch cubes
- 1 green bell pepper, seeds and stem removed, cut into ½-inch cubes
- 4 garlic cloves finely chopped
- 1 large onion cut into ½-inch cubes
- 1 teaspoon salt
- ½ teaspoon fresh ground black pepper
- 1 cup green beans, ends removed, cut into 1-inch-long pieces
- 2 cups tomatoes peeled, seeded and chopped into small cubes
- 1 cup marinara sauce
- 1 tablespoon basil thinly sliced
- 1 tablespoon chopped parsley

Directions

1. Preheat the oven to 400°F.
2. In a large roasting pan, mix the eggplant, zucchini, yellow squash, red and green peppers, onion and garlic. Season with salt and pepper. Pour olive oil over vegetables and mix to coat.
3. Bake the vegetables for 20 minutes.
4. Pour the marinara sauce into an ovenproof deep baking dish.
5. Arrange in layers the baked vegetables, green beans and chopped tomatoes including basil and parsley on each layer, finishing with the tomatoes on top. Bake the ratatouille for a half hour.

Tip

You can sprinkle a Parmesan / mozzarella mixture or crumbled feta cheese on top and broil for 5 minutes or until golden brown, being careful not to burn. Pasta, rice or bread make a nice accompaniment.

Serving Suggestions

Serve warm or at room temperature with fresh basil and parsley on top.

Stuffed Vine Leaves

(Greek - *Dolmas*)

Prep Time: 10 Min | Cook Time: 30 Min | Total Time: 40 Min

Yields 36 Dolmas

A hearty rice and lentil blend cooked with onions, dill and mint wrapped in tender grapevine leaves.

Amount & Ingredients

- ½ cup dried lentils picked over & soaked for 30 minutes in water
- ½ cup long grain white rice soaked for 30 minutes in water
- 3 tablespoons olive oil
- ½ cup white onion finely chopped
- 2 green onions finely chopped
- 3 garlic cloves minced
- 1 large tomato peeled, seeded and diced
- ½ cup pine nuts
- ⅓ cup fresh dill chopped
- ⅓ cup fresh mint chopped
- ¼ cup parsley chopped
- 1 teaspoon salt
- ½ teaspoon pepper freshly ground
- 36 brine-packed grape leaves
- ½ cup olive oil
- ¼ cup fresh lemon juice

For Serving:

- 2 cups Greek yogurt for serving
- 2 lemons cut into wedges for serving

Directions

1. In a sauté pan over medium heat, add 3 tablespoons olive oil and the white and green onions. Sauté for 6-8 minutes. Add garlic and sauté for 30 seconds more. Remove from heat.
2. Drain the rice and add it to the onion mixture along with the drained lentils, tomatoes, pine nuts, dill, mint and parsley. Season with salt and pepper. Mix it well.
3. Rinse the grape leaves and put them in a pot of boiling water over medium heat and boil for 15 minutes. Drain and rinse under cold water. Cut off any tough stems.
4. Place the leaves on a work surface, smooth side down.
5. Place about 1 teaspoon of filling near the stem end of each leaf.
6. Fold the stem end over the filling.
7. Fold the sides over the stem end and then roll the leaf into a cylinder. Do not roll too tightly. The rice will swell during cooking.
8. Place the grape leaf cylinder seam side down in a wide sauté pan.
9. Repeat with the remaining leaves and filling placing the *Dolmas* snugly in a single layer.

10. Pour the oil and lemon over the *Dolmas*. Add hot water to cover.
11. Place a heavy plate on top of the *Dolmas* to immobilize them.
12. Bring to a simmer over medium heat; cover and reduce heat to low.
13. Cook until the filling is tender (about 45 minutes).
14. Remove from heat, uncover and carefully remove the plate.
15. Transfer the *Dolmas* to a platter.

Tip You can freeze the *Dolmas* before you cook them and later, cook them as needed.

Serving Suggestions Serve at room temperature with Greek yogurt and lemon wedges. This recipe can also be served as a main vegetarian dish or as a side.

Zucchini Bikini Soufflé

with Feta

Prep Time: 20 Min | Cook Time: 30 Min | Total Time: 50 Min

Serves 6

This aromatic soufflé will elevate your guests' taste buds to new satisfying heights. Zucchini is the star of this soufflé, and will help you look good in your new bathing suit.

Amount & Ingredients

- 5 medium zucchini shredded
- 2 teaspoons salt
- 4 tablespoons olive oil
- 1 medium onion finely chopped
- 1 leek finely chopped
- ¾ cup all-purpose flour
- 2 teaspoons baking powder
- ½ cup Greek yogurt
- 1 teaspoon Dijon mustard
- 1 cup feta cheese crumbled
- ½ cup grated Gruyere cheese
- 4 eggs separated, lightly beaten
- 2 tablespoons fresh mint finely chopped
- 2 tablespoons fresh dill finely chopped
- 2 tablespoons Italian parsley (flat leaf parsley) finely chopped
- ½ teaspoon freshly ground white pepper

Directions

1. Place grated zucchini in a colander. Sprinkle with salt and toss it lightly. Let it stand for 30 minutes.
2. Then, squeeze out as much liquid as possible by pushing the zucchini down in the colander.
3. In a large sauce pan over medium heat, add the olive oil, onion and leeks. Sauté for 5-7 minutes. Add the flour and cook for 2-3 minutes more. Remove from heat and stir in the zucchini, yogurt, mustard, cheese, baking powder, lightly beaten egg yolks, mint, dill and parsley.
4. Beat egg whites in a clean bowl until stiff and fold them gently into the zucchini mixture.
5. Add the pepper and spoon the mixture into 6 greased ramekins or a large casserole dish.
6. Arrange the ramekins on baking tray and bake for 25-30 minutes until the contents are golden brown and fluffy.

Tip

If you are using a casserole dish, bake about 45-50 minutes.

Serving Suggestions

It's best to have your guests seated before you remove this dish from the oven so they can take full advantage of the soufflé's fluffiness. You can serve this as a first course, a side dish, or a light supper with a green salad.

Chapter 9

Sides, Sandwiches & Sauces

You Taught Us How to Eat

While traveling through Europe, Africa, and North and South America, I discovered many new dishes and cooking techniques.

One night as I was about to close my restaurant, Monopolio, in Syros, Greece. I went to the bar for a drink and an unusual customer caught my attention.

CUSTOMER
How you doing?

STEFANIA
Pretty good after a 12-hour shift.

CUSTOMER
Those potatoes you serve are the best ever.

STEFANIA
Thanks. I'm happy you like them.

CUSTOMER
I write for a well-known food magazine in the States.

STEFANIA
Really?

CUSTOMER
I don't know if you're willing to do this, but it would really help me win the annual company writing contest if you told me how you came up with such a wonderful recipe.

STEFANIA
Well, I guess... It was a very special Christmas. We decided to spend the holidays with Aliki, my husband Francisco's older sister. After several days of driving from Greece through Europe, our two children, Anna, 9, and Alexandros, 10, were anxious to feel the warmth of Aliki's home. We finally arrived on the afternoon of Christmas Eve.

Stefania smiles when she remembers...

FLASHBACK TO IRELAND 1979

The Volvo sputters as it strains going up the long narrow snow-covered driveway.

ALEXANDROS
This old tub gonna make it?

ANNA
Don't worry. It'll be fun walking in the snow.

To the kids, the house on top of a rolling hill outside of Dublin looks like a mini-castle.

ANNA
It's Shangri-La.

We slide into a parking space next to the house, grab our bags and approach the vintage wooden front door which is decorated with a large holly wreath.

Before we can knock, the door swings open. There's Aliki and John, her husband, sporting big welcoming smiles. The rest of the family anxiously waits behind them.

ALIKI'S FAMILY
Hi! Merry Christmas. Happy holidays. Great to see you!

We can't get in the door without each family member giving us a kiss and big hug. In the background, a quartet sings a bouncy Christmas carol. Aliki always makes us feel at home, throws us a party and stuffs her house with seasonal goodies.

We timed our arrival perfectly because-

ALIKI
It's time to enjoy four o'clock tea.

ALEXANDROS
Great! I could use something to warm me up.

We relax in beautiful antique furniture in front of a fireplace that has a blazing fire. Across the room, a well decorated seven foot Christmas tree brightens spirits.

ALIKI
Before we have tea, there's a Christmas tradition to uphold.

ANNA
Light the candle? We must light it.

JOHN
You're right. Would you like the honor?

ANNA
Can I? Please!

Aliki places the Christmas candle in a front window, and hands Anna a match. Anna carefully lights the candle.

ALIKI
It's now officially Christmas Eve.

Tricks, their excited Jack Russel Terrier, darts into the room and knocks his box of treats off a nearby coffee table. He picks a treat off the floor and starts dancing on his back legs as he devours the treat.

JOHN
Tricks, that's your Christmas present. The only one! Savor it.

FRANCISCO
What's for dinner? Pheasant, Woodcock, -

ALIKI
If you want that, grab the gun on the wall, bundle up and take a hike. Otherwise it's goose tonight.

FRANCISCO
Well... OK. Cook your goose.

ALIKI
Thought so. Tomorrow it's turkey.

STEFANIA
We are going to have your special potatoes tonight?

ALIKI
Of course. It wouldn't be Christmas Eve without them.

STEFANIA
Fantastic! Can't wait.

ALIKI
Come on. You can help me with them in the kitchen.

Aliki was a terrific cook, and because she traveled the world, she was able to enhance her expert culinary skills in a variety of exotic ways. We saunter into the kitchen.

ALIKI
Since we eat many potatoes in Ireland, we've had to develop some special recipes (see page 175).

STEFANIA
Yours is the best. Maybe someday you'll trust me, and share it.

ALIKI
(compassionately)
Stefania, my sister-in-law, I trusted you with my brother... Of course, I'll trust you with our family potato recipe.

BACK TO MONOPOLIO RESTAURANT

The restaurant is empty now except for Stefania and the one customer she's speaking with.

STEFANIA
So that's how I got the recipe. Of course, I added my own twist.

CUSTOMER
Wow! What a great story. You certainly have a menu infused with world flavors.

STEFANIA
It's been a long journey.

CUSTOMER
What kind of life philosophy do you use to keep reinventing your menu?

STEFANIA
My philosophy is simple, "Have Spatula - Will Travel."

CUSTOMER
Cool. I've even heard customers saying, "She taught us how to eat."

STEFANIA
That's really nice to hear that their palates have been broadened. Thanks.

CUSTOMER
No... Thank you! I'll send you a copy of my winning contest entry.

See recipe on page 175.

Gotta Get It Biscuit

with Feta and Yogurt

Prep Time: 20 Min **Cook Time:** 25 Min **Total Time:** 45 Min

Yields 20 Biscuits

These flakey biscuits are an excellent side to almost any meal. If you're craving a savory snack, a tangy moist biscuit makes a satisfying choice.

Amount & Ingredients

- 1¼ cups Greek yogurt
- 1 cup olive oil
- 2 eggs
- 1 tablespoon salt
- 1 tablespoon fresh thyme finely chopped
- 2½ cups self-rising flour
- 1¼ cups crumbled feta cheese

Directions

1. Preheat your oven to 375°F.
2. In a mixing bowl, combine yogurt, olive oil, eggs, feta cheese, salt and thyme.
3. Add flour to the yogurt mixture, stirring to combine.
4. Place dough on a floured working surface.
5. Knead 3-4 times. If needed, add more flour. With floured hands, press dough into a thick rectangle.
6. Cut dough with a 1½-2 inch round cutter and place each piece on a lightly greased baking sheet.
7. Bake at 375°F for 25 minutes.

Tip

For additional flavor, you can add chopped Kalamata olives to the biscuit mixture. If you do not have self-rising flour, you can add 2 teaspoons of baking powder and ½ teaspoon of baking soda to the flour and mix well.

Serving Suggestions

You can serve this with olive oil infused with fresh herbs.

Greek on Weck Sandwich

Rolls:	Prep Time: 4 Hr	Cook Time: 25 Min	Total Time: 4 Hr 25 Min
Turkey:	Prep Time: 15 Min	Cook Time: 70 Min	Total Time: 1 Hr 25 Min
Hummus:	Prep Time: 15 Min	Cook Time: 60 Min	Total Time: 1 Hr 15 Min

Serves 8

This scrumptious sandwich is a variation of the famous "Roast Beef on Weck" sandwich which is served mostly in the Buffalo, New York area. In Buffalo, "Beef on Weck" rivals "Buffalo Wings" and pizza as the most popular food.

The German *kümmelweck* roll gives the sandwich its name and unique flavor. The word, *kümmelweck*, is derived from *kümmel*, which is the German word for caraway and *weck* which means "roll." Both caraway seeds and large grains of salt are roasted on the top of the roll. In western New York this roast beef sandwich is usually served with horseradish and a dill pickle spear.

The version presented here replaces beef with turkey. The recipe infuses the Greek flavors of hummus and Kalamata olives along with tomatoes, onions and cabbage for an innovative Mediterranean treat.

Amount & Ingredients

Rolls:

- 3 teaspoons active dry yeast
- 1¼ cups lukewarm water
- 3 tablespoons vegetable oil
- 1 tablespoon honey
- 2 large egg whites
- ½ teaspoon salt
- 3½ cups bread flour
- 1 tablespoon water
- 1 teaspoon salt flakes such as Maldon for sprinkling
- 1 teaspoon caraway seeds for sprinkling

Hummus:

- 1½ cups dried chickpeas (soaked in cold water overnight)
- ⅓ cup lemon juice
- ⅓ cup water
- 1 teaspoon lemon zest
- 1 teaspoon cumin
- 1 teaspoon coriander
- ½ teaspoon smoked paprika
- ¼ teaspoon red pepper flakes
- 2 tablespoons tahini
- 2 garlic cloves
- 2 roasted piquillo peppers
- 1 teaspoon salt
- ½ cup extra virgin olive oil

Amount & Ingredients

Roast Turkey:

1 5-6 pounds deboned turkey breast, halved, skin on
3 tablespoons olive oil
3 garlic cloves, minced
1 tablespoon sage
1 tablespoon rosemary finely chopped
1 tablespoon thyme finely chopped
2 teaspoons salt
1 teaspoon black pepper freshly ground

Sandwich:

1 white onion thinly sliced into rings
2 breakfast tomatoes thinly sliced
2 cups white cabbage shredded thinly
2 cups Kalamata olives thinly sliced
8 slices Provolone cheese
8 dill pickle spears
8 teaspoons horseradish mustard

Greek on Weck Sandwich

(continued)

Directions

To Prepare the Rolls:

1. In a medium bowl, combine the yeast and ¼ cup lukewarm water. Set aside to proof (about 5-10 minutes).
2. In the same bowl, add the remaining water, 2 tablespoons oil, honey and 1 egg white. Mix to combine.
3. In a large mixing bowl, combine flour and salt.
4. Add the yeast mixture to the flour and mix it until the dough becomes smooth.
5. Place the dough onto a lightly floured work surface and knead it for 5-10 minutes adding only as much additional flour as necessary to keep the dough from sticking.
6. Put the dough in a clean large greased bowl. Cover the bowl with plastic wrap and set aside in a dark place at warm room temperature. Allow the dough to rise until it has doubled in size (about 1½ - 2 hours).
7. Punch dough down using your fists. Cover the bowl again and let the dough rise a second time (about 30-60 minutes).
8. Place the dough onto a lightly floured work surface and divide it into 8 equal pieces (about 17 ounces each). Shape each piece into a smooth round roll about 4 inches in diameter.
9. Place rolls on a parchment-lined baking sheet. Space them apart leaving enough space for them to rise and expand.
10. Cover the rolls loosely with a clean towel and let them rise again (about 1 hour).
11. Preheat the oven to 425°F.
12. In a small bowl, mix the leftover egg white with one tablespoon water and then brush this lightly over each roll top.
13. With a sharp knife make slits on the roll tops in a tic-tac-toe pattern.
14. Mix the salt flakes and caraway seeds. Sprinkle this mixture over each roll top. Spray the roll tops lightly with water.
15. Bake the rolls for five minutes. Then open the oven door and quickly spray the tops with water again.
16. Bake 20 minutes more until the rolls are lightly brown and crisp.

To Prepare the Turkey:

1. Preheat the oven to 400°F.
2. Under cold water rinse the turkey breast and pat it dry with paper towels.
3. Combine olive oil, garlic, sage, rosemary and thyme.
4. Rub the turkey breast with salt and pepper.
5. Loosen the breast skin by gently placing your hand between the skin and the meat.
6. Spread the garlic mixture under the skin and rub the leftover in the cavity.
7. Place the turkey breast into a roasting pan.
8. Cover the breast with foil and bake for 40 minutes.
9. Remove the foil and bake for 30 more minutes or until golden brown.
10. If using a thermometer, insert it into the thickest part of the turkey. When the thermometer registers 160°F, the turkey is done.
11. Remove the turkey and let it rest for 15 minutes before carving.

To Prepare the Hummus:

1. Strain the chickpeas.
2. Boil the chickpeas in a covered medium pot for about 1 hour until soft and tender. Then, strain the chickpeas and place them in a food processor with the rest of the ingredients. Liquidize.
3. If the mixture is too thick, add a small amount of water and liquidize again.

Tip

In place of the turkey you can substitute thinly sliced chicken, lamb or beef for a variation. For the hummus, you can substitute canned chickpeas rinsed thoroughly.

Serving Suggestions

Serve the sandwiches as soon as possible after the rolls come from the oven. Slice each roll horizontally. Generously cover the bottom half of the roll with the hummus. Place the following ingredients one at a time over the hummus: olives, cheese, thinly sliced turkey, tomato, onion, cabbage and a dill pickle spear. On the other roll half spread the horseradish mustard. Close the sandwich. Cut the sandwich in half. Enjoy!

Israeli Couscous

with Beetroot and Peas

Prep Time: 10 Min **Cook Time:** 1 Hr **Total Time:** 1 Hr 10 Min

Serves 4

A colorful hearty low-calorie side dish that accompanies seafood well.

Amount & Ingredients

- 2 teaspoons olive oil
- 2 shallots cut into small cubes
- 1 garlic clove finely chopped
- 1¼ cups water
- 1 cup whole wheat couscous (or regular)
- 1 medium red beetroot
- ½ cup fresh or frozen green peas
- 2 tablespoons Italian parsley finely chopped

Directions

1. Preheat oven to 375°F.
2. Wash the beetroot and wrap it with aluminum foil.
3. Bake the beetroot for 45-60 minutes until tender.
4. In a small sauce pan over medium heat, put the olive oil and shallots. Sauté for 2 minutes. Add the garlic and sauté for 30 seconds more.
5. Add the 1¼ cups of water, and bring it to a boil. Add the couscous and cook for 8 minutes stirring occasionally. Add the peas and cook another 2 minutes.
6. Remove the beetroot from the oven and put it in cold water until cool enough to touch. Peel the skin and chop the beet into small cubes.
7. Add the beetroot cubes and half of the parsley to the couscous mixture.

Tip You can add some sautéed kale for additional flavor.

Serving Suggestions Serve this dish warm and sprinkle the parsley on top.

Stefania's Roasted Potatoes

Prep Time: 10 Min **Cook Time:** 1 Hr **Total Time:** 1 Hr 10 Min

Serves 4

This side dish goes well with poultry, beef or fish. It was a favorite at our Christmas meals in Ireland and at my restaurants in Syros, Greece.

Amount & Ingredients

6 medium size baked potatoes
4 garlic cloves minced
1 teaspoon chopped fresh thyme
1 teaspoon chopped fresh rosemary
1 teaspoon chopped fresh sage
½ cup extra virgin olive oil
1 teaspoon salt
½ teaspoon black pepper freshly ground

Garnish:

1 tablespoon chopped parsley

Directions

1. Preheat oven to 375°F.
2. Peel potatoes.
3. Cut potatoes into 4-6 pieces each.
4. Put potatoes in a large saucepan and cover with water adding 1 teapoon of salt.
5. Bring to a boil. As soon as water starts to boil, strain the potatoes through a colander.
6. Let the potatoes dry for a few minutes.
7. In a small food processor, add garlic, thyme, rosemary, sage and olive oil.
8. Puree this mixture.
9. Place potatoes in a roasting pan in a single layer.
10. Pour the oil mixture over the potatoes covering them thoroughly.
11. Bake the potatoes for about 1 hour until golden brown.

Tip

You can add 2 cups of chopped fresh tomatoes to the oil mixture and then bake the potatoes.

Serving Suggestions

Put potatoes on a serving plate with chopped parsley on top.

Tantalizing Tartar Sauce

with Celery Root

Prep Time: 15 Min | **Cook Time:** 0 Min | **Total Time:** 15 Min

Yields 2¾ cups

This sauce is a great complement for salmon or crab cakes.

Amount & Ingredients

- ½ cup light mayonnaise
- ½ cup light sour cream
- 1 tablespoon Dijon mustard
- 2 tablespoons small pickled cornichons, diced
- ½ tablespoon lemon juice
- 1 cup celery root grated
- ½ teaspoon salt
- ½ teaspoon Worcestershire sauce

Directions

1. Mix all ingredients together in a bowl.
2. Cover the bowl with plastic wrap, and place in refrigerator.

Tip

This sauce is best if refrigerated for 1 hour before use. Also, it can be accented with minced capers and chopped dill.

Serving Suggestions

This simple dip can accompany all fish and shellfish or any battered seafood or barbecued fish. With its zingy flavor, it can be used as a sandwich spread in place of ordinary mundane mayonnaise.

Chapter 10

Tempting Treats

Aunt Anna's Just-in-Time Spartan Muffins

Maria, a fourteen-year-old, attractive Greek girl, stands by a rustic wooden kitchen table intently reading a cookbook. She wears older clothes handed down from her parents. They're the antithesis of "hip."

Her austere home located in Kato Manna, Greece is on the Aegean island of Syros. It's Easter season, and the cupboard is practically barren. Two cans look lonely next to a half sack of flour. A few odd jars of rose marmalade, lemon preserves, olive oil and baking powder adorn the counter.

There's a knock on the door. Excited, Maria rushes to the door to greet her two good friends, Phoebe and Eleni, fourteen and fifteen respectively.

ELENI
How are you?

MARIA
Great, and you?

ELENI
Fine, and do we have news for you.

Maria's eyes widen.

PHOEBE
Go on, Eleni. Tell her.

ELENI
We invited Alexandros to visit you this afternoon.

Maria's body begins to tremble.

MARIA
Oh no. Oh no! He's coming here?

ELENI
What's wrong? I thought you liked him. Why aren't you saying, "Bravo?" He's the hottest guy around, and-

PHOEBE
She's flipped out. I told her not to go scuba diving alone. She's got water on the brain.

Maria, in a panic, sprints to the kitchen, and starts rummaging through the cupboards. Cans fly. A flour mist billows from the shelves engulfing her.

ELENI
What the heck you doing?

Maria turns to her friends, her face covered with blotches of flower.

MARIA
We've been fasting. It's Lent. There's no food in the house. He'll know for sure we're poor.

PHOEBE
Who cares? He's got to like you for who you are.

Aunt Anna, an enduring, but clever relative, stands unnoticed behind the girls smiling. She approaches the flustered group.

AUNT ANNA
Girls, girls, girls let's not get our pony tails in a panic.

Maria with glassy eyes, stares at her aunt.

MARIA
Aunt Anna, I'm really in trouble.

AUNT ANNA
Now, now, my pretty niece. Don't worry. Aunt Anna always has a solution.

MARIA
Like what? He'll be here any second, and we don't have anything.

AUNT ANNA
How 'bout we throw together some of my "Just-In-Time Spartan Muffins?" We've got to be shrewd - use items from around the house.

MARIA
But what'll we do for ingredients?

AUNT ANNA
Just let me handle things. Phoebe get a couple of oranges from the garden. Eleni get that rack of dried grapes and walnuts from the shed.

MARIA
But-

AUNT ANNA
Maria, you help me in the kitchen.

Aunt Anna claps her hands several times vigorously.

AUNT ANNA
Come on now girls, get moving. We've got work to do.

Phoebe and Eleni rush out to the garden on their gastronomic treasure hunt. Aunt Anna grabs the flour from the cupboard and snatches a jar of baking powder.

Maria's friends dart back into the kitchen with their newly found culinary gems and the cooking frenzy begins. The girls, with Aunt Anna's assistance, scurry around the kitchen, throw a blue and white tablecloth over an old-fashioned table. They set the table with plates and cups handed down from Grandma Sophia.

Soon the small house fills with the wonderful aroma of muffins baking.

There's a knock on the door. The girls stare at each other.

ALL THE GIRLS
He's here!

ELENI
Don't just stand there. Answer the door!

A metamorphosis overcomes Maria. She wipes her face and with sophistication struts to the front door. She slowly opens the door.

MARIA
(confidently)
Well, hello Alexandros. Won't you come in.

ALEXANDROS
Sure. Good to see you.

Phoebe and Eleni give the new arrival an amorous smile.

PHOEBE / ELENI
(giggling)
Hi, Alexandros.

Alexandros enters the house. The muffin bouquet now permeates the air. It's a young lovers' aromatherapy.

Alexandros raises his nose and begins sniffing profusely.

ALEXANDROS
Hey. What's that great smell?

MARIA
Oh, it's really nothing. Just some muffins I whipped up. Let's sit at the dining table.

The muffins are stacked in a pyramid in the center of the table still steaming. Without hesitation Alexandros grabs one as he sits down, and takes a huge bite.

ALEXANDROS
Wow! These are gifts from Aphrodite.

His eyes pop as he stares at Maria passionately.

ALEXANDROS
I didn't know you could bake. Must have taken lots of time.

MARIA
No, it was easy.

Phoebe and Eleni snicker.

ALEXANDROS
(passionately)
I'll have to stop by more often... when you're completely alone!

Phoebe's and Eleni's jaws drop.

See recipe on page 187.

Athena Anglaise

Greek Crème Anglaise

Prep Time: 5 Min | **Cook Time:** 10 Min | **Total Time:** 15 Min

Yields 3½ cups

This simple, but elegant custard sauce is delightful over fruit.

Amount & Ingredients

- 6 egg yolks
- ⅔ cup sugar
- 1½ cups hot whole milk
- 1 tablespoon butter
- 1 vanilla bean, split lengthwise
- 2 tablespoons dark rum, cognac or mastika (or Mastiha) liqueur

Directions

1. In a small bowl, whisk the egg yolks with the sugar. Slowly pour the hot milk into the egg mixture stirring constantly. Transfer this mixture to a sauce pan and cook over medium heat stirring constantly.
2. Scrape the vanilla bean seeds into the mixture and whisk to combine.
3. Cook, stirring constantly, until custard is thick enough to coat the back of a spoon. Do not let it boil.
4. Pour the custard through a sieve.
5. Stir in the butter and rum (cognac or mastika).
6. Refrigerate for 1 hour.

Tip

To have real Greek flavor, substitute mastika for rum.

Serving Suggestions

After the sauce cools, spoon it over fresh fruit.

Aunt Anna's

Just-In-Time Spartan Muffins

Prep Time: 10 Min **Cook Time:** 40 Min **Total Time:** 50 Min

Serves 4

My Aunt Anna was like my second mother. She often prepared these delicious inexpensive muffins spontaneously for me when my friends decided to have an impromptu party (see story on page 181).

Additionally, baking with olive oil is a healthy alternative. You'll be pleasantly surprised that there is no hint of olive oil in the taste, and the oil helps produce a moist result. These tasty and filling muffins make a perfect breakfast side or snack. Since they're not overly sweet, they're a great partner to jams, jellies, or honey.

Since they're easy and quick to prepare, they're ideal when you have unexpected guests. Plus, these low-cost morsels are perfect if you're on a Spartan budget.

Amount & Ingredients

- ¾ cup walnuts
- 2 cups all-purpose flour
- 1 teaspoon baking powder
- ½ teaspoon baking soda
- ¼ teaspoon salt
- 1 teaspoon cinnamon
- ½ teaspoon ground cloves
- ¾ cup raisins
- 1 cup powdered sugar
- ¾ cup extra virgin olive oil
- 1 cup freshly squeezed orange juice
- 2 tablespoons orange zest

Directions

1. Preheat the oven to 350°F.
2. Place the walnuts on sheet pan.
3. Bake for 5 minutes and set aside.
4. Line a cupcake pan with twelve paper liners and spray them with non-stick cooking spray.
5. In a medium bowl, add flour, baking powder, baking soda, salt, cinnamon and cloves.
6. Mix to combine all ingredients.
7. Add raisins, walnuts and sugar. Mix to combine.
8. With a spoon make a hole in the flour. Add the olive oil, orange juice and orange zest. Thoroughly combine all the ingredients.
9. Scoop the batter into the prepared 12 cupcake pan.
10. Bake for 30 minutes or until a toothpick comes out clean.
11. Cool for 10 minutes on a wire rack.

Tip

When using the muffins as a dessert, you can top each muffin with your own frosting.

Serving Suggestions

These muffins can accompany many foods but can also be a stand-alone snack during a coffee or tea break.

On a cold day, they are perfect with a cup of hot chocolate and conversely on a summer afternoon they're great with a scoop of your favorite ice cream.

Creamy Custard Pie

(Greek - *Bougatsa*)

Prep Time: 1 Hr **Cook Time:** 30 Min **Total Time:** 1 Hr 30 Min

Serves 8

This classic dessert or snack is often available in Greek bakeries and pastry shops. The tasty combination of creamy custard over a crispy crust makes a tempting treat.

Amount & Ingredients

- 4½ cups whole milk
- 1 cup sugar
- ½ cup fine semolina flour
- 2 tablespoons cornstarch
- 2 teaspoons cold milk
- 4 whole eggs
- 1 tablespoon lemon zest
- 1 teaspoon vanilla extract
- 2 tablespoons butter cut into bites
- ⅛ teaspoon salt
- 12 sheets filo pastry
- 1 cup butter, melted
- ½ cup olive oil

Directions

To Prepare the Custard:

1. In a medium pot, heat the milk over medium heat but do not boil.
2. Reduce heat to low and gradually sprinkle into the pot the semolina flour while constantly stirring.
3. In a medium bowl, beat the eggs, sugar and vanilla.
4. In a small bowl, mix the cornstarch with cold milk and add this to the pot with the custard while stirring.
5. Add the egg mixture to the custard and stir constantly over low heat for about 2-3 minutes until it reaches a creamy consistency.
6. Remove the custard mixture from heat and stir the in lemon zest, butter and salt.
7. Allow the mixture to cool completely stirring occasionally to keep the custard from forming a skin on top.

To Prepare the Pie:

1. Preheat oven to 350°F.
2. Combine the melted butter with the olive oil.
3. Brush a round 9-inch baking dish with butter.
4. Place 1 filo sheet at the bottom of the baking dish and brush it with the butter mixture.
5. Repeat with the next 7 filo sheets brushing each sheet well with the melted butter.
6. Add the custard filling on top of the prepared filo sheets and fold the excess filo that overlaps the baking dish in over the custard.

7. Top the filing with the remaining filo sheets, brushing each one with butter.
8. Use a knife or scissors to trim the top sheets to the size of the pan.
9. Spray the top lightly with water. Bake for about 30-40 minutes until top is golden brown.

Tip

You can also make this recipe as individual pies by cutting the filo into smaller pieces. Roll the filo pieces up like spring rolls.

Serving Suggestions

Sprinkle the top with icing sugar and cinnamon. It is better if served warm.

Lemon Meringue Pie

with a Nutty Crust

Prep Time: 30 Min   Cook Time: 45 Min   Total Time: 1 Hr 15 Min

Serves 10

This is my son's favorite dessert. When he returned from school in England, he brought me a cookbook as a present. He made sure his favorite dessert was included. Presented here is my version of my son Alexandros' beloved sweet. The hazelnuts add a nice crunch.

Amount & Ingredients

Pastry:

- ½ cup hazelnuts toasted and husked
- 1½ cups all-purpose flour
- ½ teaspoon salt
- ½ cup powdered sugar
- ½ cup unsalted butter room temperature
- 1 large egg yolk
- 2 tablespoons water
- 1 tablespoon lemon zest
- 1 teaspoon vanilla extract

Filling:

- 5 large egg yolks
- 1 cup sugar
- 4 tablespoons cornstarch
- ¼ teaspoon salt
- 1½ cups water
- ½ cup fresh lemon juice
- 2 tablespoons lemon zest
- 2 tablespoons butter

Meringue:

- 6 egg whites
- ½ teaspoon crème of tartar
- 1 cup powdered sugar
- 1 teaspoon vanilla extract

Directions

To Prepare the Pastry:

1. Position an oven rack in the center of the oven.
2. Preheat oven to 350°F.
3. In a food processor, add hazelnuts and grind finely. Add flour, salt, sugar and blend. Add butter, egg yolk, water and vanilla. Pulse a few times just until the dough forms moist clumps.
4. Place the dough on a lightly floured surface. Gather the dough into a ball shape. Then flatten it into a round shape. Wrap it in plastic and refrigerate for 30 minutes.
5. Roll out dough between sheets of wax paper to a 12-inch round piece turning over occasionally to lift, and smooth the wax paper.
6. Peel off the top sheet of paper using the bottom paper as an aid. Lift dough and invert into 9-inch diameter glass pie dish. Peel off paper. Press the dough gently into the dish. Fold the overhang under crimping with your hands to form a decorative edge.

7. Pierce the crust all over with fork. Chill 15 minutes. Line the crust with foil. Fill with dried beans or pie weights. Bake crust for 15 minutes. Remove foil and beans. Bake until crust is pale golden (about 20 minutes longer). Transfer the crust to rack and cool completely.

To Prepare the Filling:

1. Reduce oven to 325°F.
2. In a small bowl, beat egg yolks with a fork. In a two-quart sauce pan, mix sugar, cornstarch and salt. Stir in the water gradually.
3. Cook over medium heat, stirring constantly until mixture thickens and just begins to boil.
4. Whisk in at least half of the hot mixture into the egg yolk.
5. Stir the egg mixture back into hot mixture in the sauce pan.
6. Boil and stir for 1 minute, or until the mixture thickens. Remove from heat.
7. Whisk in butter, lemon juice and zest. Pour into pie crust.

To Prepare the Meringue:

1. Beat egg whites and crème of tartar with an electric mixer on high speed until foamy.
2. Beat in sugar 1 tablespoon at a time. Continue beating until stiff and glossy. Beat in vanilla.
3. Spoon onto hot pie filling. Spread over filling carefully sealing the meringue to edge of crust to prevent shrinking or weeping.
4. Bake 10-15 minutes, or until meringue is light brown.
5. Cool for 2 hours before serving.

Tip

The pastry can be made 2-3 days ahead of time. Walnuts or almonds can be used instead of hazelnuts.

Serving Suggestions

Serve this pie chilled or at room temperature with candied lemons slices.

Mama's Lava Soufflé

Prep Time: 20 Min | Cook Time: 25 Min | Total Time: 45 Min

Serves 6

You may think this elegant sweet needs special care, but it's easy to make. This light and fluffy morsel erupts with flavor as if it were a taste from heaven. The best part is that you can create and enjoy it at home.

Amount & Ingredients

- 3 tablespoons unsalted butter, plus more for the ramekins
- 3 tablespoons all-purpose flour
- 1¼ cup whole milk
- 8 ounces bittersweet chocolate, melted
- 3 large egg yokes
- 2 tablespoons Grand Marnier Liqueur
- 1 cup sugar, plus more for the ramekins
- 2 teaspoons vanilla extract
- 8 large egg whites
- 1 pinch crème of tartar

Garnish:

- 6 ounces Grand Marnier Liqueur
- 3 tablespoons confectioner sugar

Directions

1. Place an oven rack in the lower ⅓ of the oven. Preheat oven to 400°F.
2. Butter 6 ramekins. Sprinkle with sugar. Shake off the excess. Place them on a baking sheet.
3. In a medium sauce pan, melt butter over medium heat. Add flour, stirring until the mixture smells nutty and is lightly golden (about 1 minute).
4. Pour in milk whisking constantly until the consistency of the mixture is similar to a thin pudding (about 2 minutes).
5. Whisk in the chocolate mixture until smooth. Remove from heat and set aside.
6. In a bowl, combine the egg yolks, sugar, liqueur and vanilla. Beat until frothy (about 5 minutes).
7. Fold the egg mixture into the melted chocolate and combine.
8. Beat the egg whites and crème of tartar using an electric mixer on medium-high speed until stiff peaks form (about 4-5 minutes).
9. Fold a third of the egg whites into the chocolate mixture and gently combine. Then slowly fold in the remaining egg whites and gently combine.
10. Fill the prepared ramekins ¾ full with the prepared batter.
11. Bake without opening the oven door until the soufflés rise (about 18-22 minutes).
12. Remove from the oven, and serve immediately.

Tip To melt the chocolate, place it in the microwave in an oven-safe bowl. Another method is to utilize a double boiler on the stove.

Serving Suggestions Dust the soufflé tops with confectioner sugar. Drizzle the tops with Grand Marnier Liqueur for enhanced aroma and flavor.

My Irish Christmas Pudding

Prep Time: 30 Min **Cook Time:** 3 Hr **Total Time:** 3 Hr 30 Min

Serves 8

During Christmas season, I have made many trips to Ireland to visit my relatives and this recipe was always a favorite. But, it isn't the traditional Irish Christmas pudding recipe since I've given it the Greek touch. It's delicious and easy to prepare. The brandy, ginger and orange give a Christmas feeling that will certainly excite guests. For an extra kick, accompany the pudding with the brandy butter described below.

Amount & Ingredients

Pudding:

- 1 cup sultanas
- ½ cup raisins
- 4 oz. dates, pits removed
- 1 orange's zest and juice
- 3 pieces of ginger, stemmed
- ¼ cup dried sour cherries
- ½ cup dried cranberries
- 7 tablespoons suet (kidney fat) or vegetable shortening
- 1 teaspoon ground ginger
- 1 cup all-purpose flour
- 1 teaspoon baking powder
- 1 teaspoon cinnamon
- ¼ teaspoon ground cloves
- ⅔ cup brown sugar
- 2 tablespoons quality brandy
- ¼ teaspoon salt
- 8 oz. ciabatta bread
- 1 large egg
- ⅔ cup whole milk
- 1 tablespoon butter

Brandy Butter:

- 4 oz. soft unsalted butter
- 6 oz. icing sugar
- 3-5 tablespoons brandy or cognac

Directions

Pudding:

1. Rub butter around the inside of a 2-quart pudding bowl using a small piece of butter making sure you coat the bowl evenly.
2. Finely chop the stemmed ginger and dates. Place them in a large mixing bowl with sultanas, raisins, sour cherries and cranberries.
3. Add the suet or vegetable shortening, flour, baking powder, sugar, cinnamon, ground cloves, brandy, salt and ground ginger to the mixing bowl. Grate the zest of the orange, and add it with the orange juice into the mixing bowl.
4. Remove the crust of the ciabatta, and tear the remaining bread into chunks. Place the chunks into a food processor and blitz until you have bread crumbs. Add the crumbs to the mixing bowl and mix the contents with a wooden spoon.
5. In a small mixing bowl, beat the egg and milk together. Pour this

into the large bowl containing the rest of the ingredients. Mix everything together thoroughly.

6. Carefully pour the mixture into the greased bowl and smooth the surface so that mixture is even.
7. Tear off two greaseproof papers that are a little larger than the rim of the mixture bowl. Butter one piece on one side and place it buttered-side down on top of the mixture.
8. Top that piece with the other piece of the greaseproof paper. Then top that with a piece of aluminum foil folding the foil down around the rim of bowl. Use a string to tie them tightly in place.
9. Place a small plate in the bottom of a large sauce pan. Put the pudding bowl on top. Pour cold water into the pan until it is half way up the side of the bowl.
10. Cover with a lid and bring the water to a boil over medium-high heat. Lower the heat to low and simmer for 3 hours. Check the water level regularly adding hot water as needed to keep the level half way.
11. When the time is up, carefully lift the pudding out of the pan. You can serve it now or let it cool.

Brandy Butter:

1. Cream the butter and icing sugar.
2. Add the brandy little by little so the mixture will not curdle. If it does, don't worry. Add more icing sugar until it binds back together.

Tip

The pudding can be made one week before it is needed. The brandy butter can be made up to 5 days in advance.

Serving Suggestions

Chill until needed. Serve the pudding cold or at room temperature. Spoon brandy butter on top.

Poached Pears

in Sweet Wine

Prep Time: 15 Min **Cook Time:** 30 Min **Total Time:** 45 Min

Serves 4

Mavrodafni is a sweet and spicy Greek dessert wine. This ingredient causes the dish to shine on a cold night when an elegant presentation is desired.

Amount & Ingredients

- 4 firm, ripe pears
- 3 cups Mavrodafni sweet red wine
- 1 tablespoon orange zest
- 1 cinnamon stick
- 8 mint leaves for decoration
- 1 tablespoon cornstarch
- 2 tablespoons water
- 1 cup whipped cream for decoration

Garnish:

- 1 cup whipped cream
- ¼ cup baked almond slivers
- ¼ cup mint leaves

Directions

1. Peel the pears leaving the stem intact being careful not to blemish the flesh of the pear.
2. Slice ½ inch off the bottom of the pear to create a flat bottom.
3. Gently place the pears in a 4-quart saucepan with the orange zest and cinnamon. Pour in the wine.
4. Simmer for 20 minutes turning the pears every 5 minutes to ensure even color until the pears are cooked but still firm.
5. Remove the saucepan from heat and let it cool with pears upright in the pan.
6. Once the pears are cool, remove them from the liquid and place them on a deep serving plate.
7. Put the saucepan on medium heat and bring to boil.
8. In a small bowl, add cornstarch and water mixing them well.
9. Slowly pour the cornstarch into the saucepan and stir until the liquid has thickened.
10. Remove the saucepan from the heat and drizzle each pear with the thickened wine liquid.
11. Garnish with whipped cream and mint leaves.

Tip

If you core the cooked pear with an apple corer leaving pears whole, you can fill pears with whipped cream or Mascarpone cheese.

Serving Suggestions

Serve on dessert plates or in small bowls sprinkled with baked almonds.

Seductive Crepes

Stuffed with Yogurt, Honey and Fruit

Prep Time: 20 Min Cook Time: 25 Min Total Time: 45 Min

Makes 12 crepes

Made with light sauces and fillings, this enticing dessert suits today's passion for a healthy fare. Luscious berries cover a creamy yogurt-filled crepe that will satisfy your sweet desires.

Amount & Ingredients

Crepes:

- 1 cup all-purpose flour, sifted
- ¼ teaspoon salt
- 1 cup whole milk
- 4 large eggs

Filling:

- 1 cup Mascarpone cheese
- ½ cup non-fat Greek yogurt
- 4 tablespoons honey
- 1 tablespoon orange zest
- ⅓ cup fresh raspberries
- ⅓ cup blueberries
- ⅓ cup fresh strawberries thinly sliced

Strawberry Sauce:

- 2 cups sliced fresh strawberries
- 1 tablespoon balsamic vinegar
- ½ cup sugar
- ½ cup water
- 1 tablespoon cornstarch

Directions

To Prepare the Crepes:

1. Put all the crepe ingredients in a blender, and process into a smooth batter.
2. Cover, and refrigerate for one hour.
3. Heat to medium-high a non-stick 6-8 inch skillet, or a crepe pan.
4. When hot, spray the pan with olive oil.
5. Ladle about 2 ounces of the crepe batter into the skillet tilting the skillet to evenly coat the pan's surface with the batter.
6. Cook 1-2 minutes until the crepe's bottom is golden brown. With a spatula turn the crepe and cook the other side about 40 seconds until slightly colored.
7. Transfer the crepe to a plate and cover. Repeat the process with the remaining batter.

To Prepare the Filling:

1. In a mixing bowl, combine the Mascarpone cheese, yogurt, honey and orange zest.
2. Gently fold in the raspberries, blueberries and strawberries. Cover and refrigerate.

To Prepare the Strawberry Sauce:

1. In a small pot over medium heat, combine strawberries, sugar and balsamic vinegar. Bring to a boil. Simmer for 3-4 minutes.

2. In a small bowl, dilute the cornstarch with water. Add this to the strawberry mixture.
3. Simmer for 1-2 minutes until the mixture thickens slightly. Remove from heat.
4. When ready to serve, place the yogurt-fruit mixture evenly on one side of all 12 crepes. Then roll each crepe into a tight cylinder.

Tip You can substitute peaches and nectarines in place of the raspberries and blueberries.

Serving Suggestions Place the crepes in the center of a plate. Spoon 2 tablespoons of strawberry sauce on top. Garnish with fresh fruit and mint leaves.

Very Berry Tart

Add Zing to Your Dessert

Prep Time: 1 Hr 15 Min Cook Time: 40 Min Total Time: 1 Hr 55 Min

Serves 12

This is a great make-ahead dessert for special occasions such as a party, weekend brunch, a buffet or summer lunch. It can be made as one large tart or small individual tarts.

Amount & Ingredients

Crust:

- 8 oz. (2 sticks) unsalted butter slightly softened
- 1 cup confectioners' sugar
- 2 egg yolks plus 1 more for brushing
- 2 cups flour
- ¼ teaspoon salt
- 1 teaspoon vanilla extract

Filling:

- 1 cup fresh lemon juice (from 4-6 lemons)
- 2 oz. (4 tablespoons) unsalted butter, cut into 2 pieces
- 2 tablespoons heavy cream
- 1 cup granulated sugar
- 4 large eggs
- 2 large egg yolks
- ¼ teaspoon salt
- 1 teaspoon vanilla extract
- 2 tablespoons lemon zest

Topping:

- ½ cup sliced fresh strawberries
- ½ cup blueberries
- ½ cup raspberries
- 1 large kiwi peeled and sliced
- ¼ cup apricot preserves
- 1-2 tablespoons water

Directions

To Prepare the crust:

1. Preheat the oven to 350°F.
2. In the bowl of an electric mixer, cream butter and sugar just until mixed. Don't fluff up the mixture by incorporating air. The mixture should be smooth with no lumps of butter.
3. Add the yolks 1 at a time and process to mix just until incorporated, scraping down the bowl once. Add vanilla, flour and salt. Mix these to combine. Don't over mix.
4. Gather the dough into a ball. Wrap it in plastic and chill for 30 minutes.
5. You may use one large tart tin or several smaller tins. Roll the dough on a lightly floured surface that is slightly larger than the tart tin you decide to use to accommodate the pastry needed for the sides of the tin(s).
6. Place greaseproof paper over the top of each tin(s) and fill with baking beans. Rest this in the refrigerator for 30 minutes.
7. Bake tart(s) for 15 minutes. Lift out paper and beans. Brush the dough with beaten egg yolk. Place it back into the oven for 8-10 minutes until golden. Remove from oven and allow it to cool for 15 minutes.

To Prepare the Filling:

1. Over medium heat in a medium-sized sauce pan, heat the lemon juice, butter and cream to just under a boil. The butter should be melted. Remove from heat.
2. In a medium bowl, whisk sugar, eggs and yolks until combined. Whisk in a bit of the hot liquid and then gradually whisk in a bit more until it's all added.
3. Pour the mixture back into the sauce pan over medium heat stirring constantly with a wooden spoon. Scrape the bottom and sides of the pan. Cook on low heat until the mixture thickens (5-8 minutes).
4. Remove from heat and strain the mixture through a fine sieve. Stir in salt, vanilla and lemon zest.
5. Spoon the cream into the baked tart and smooth it evenly with a spatula.
6. Top the tart(s) with the fruits arranging them in a decorative fashion.
7. Put the apricot preserve and water in a small sauce pan. Warm it through so that it loosens up and becomes more liquified. Lightly brush the fruits to glaze.

Tip

You can freeze the tarts before baking. Later, you can bake them as needed. Also, you can top the tarts with other fresh fruits of your choice that are in season such as blackberries.

Serving Suggestions

Place the tarts on a cake stand and garnish with mint tips and/or pistachios.

Ask Chef Stefania

As a private chef, my clients and their guests often ask me questions about food preparation and culinary careers. Here are some of their questions. I hope my responses help you with some of your challenges.

Cooking Tips

1. What is your favorite ingredient to work with?

   Chef Stefania: Being from the Greek island of Syros, I enjoy working with all types of seafood. My favorite seafood is sea urchin which I prepare often. Sometimes I serve it over scrambled eggs or as a filler for an avocado half.

   Plus, I love cooking the whole fish. I season the fish simply with salt, pepper and fresh thyme attempting to bring out the fish's own flavor. After the fish comes off the grill, oven or pan, finish it with a little fresh olive oil and squeezed lemon.

2. How can I be sure the whole fish I choose is fresh?

   Chef Stefania: Buy your fish from a seafood store. The fish eyes have to be bright and clear. The skin must be firm. When you press your finger on the fish skin, it should not leave a depression. Also, there should not be a strong fishy smell.

3. Chef, often times when I cook, I follow a recipe exactly. But, the meal turns out poorly, especially when I'm trying to impress a guest. Please help me.

   Chef Stefania: Don't worry! Remember that cooking is an art, not a science. Recipes are only guidelines.

   The most important part of the process is your brain and your ability to adjust. Feel comfortable replacing ingredients with similar ones that you like.

   Also, all pans are not created equal. If you are using a cast iron pan, it will take longer to heat than an aluminum pan but it will retain its heat longer. Just adjust your cook time.

4. I love Greek and Mediterranean cuisine but sometimes I can't find the ingredients such as Mastika (I saw it was an ingredient in your Mystic Mastic Mojito). Do you have any thoughts on this?

Chef Stefania: Here are a couple of things you might try. Visit websites such as www.greekshops.com for items in general or www.yamastiha.com/home/ for Mastiha Liqueur.

Also, many communities have a Greek festival where hard-to-find items may be sold. In your favorite search engine (Google, Yahoo, Bing, iseek), enter a search term such as "greek festival (year)" to find a Greek festival in your area. Also, check The Ultimate Food Scout for more resources (see page 214).

5. How do you keep your aromatic herbs fresh?

Chef Stefania: Basil stays fresh longer at room temperature with its stems in water. For arugula, wrap it loosely in a damp paper towel. Put it in a sealable plastic bag and store it in your refrigerator.

6. When I cook cauliflower, it leaves an unpleasant smell in the house. Is there any way to avoid this?

Chef Stefania: When I boil cauliflower, I add a celery stalk to prevent the smell. Also, you can add two tablespoons of milk to make the cauliflower look brighter and whiter.

7. My kids and I love to bake. How can I get the best results?

Chef Stefania: Cooking and baking are so much fun. For the best results, use room temperature butter and eggs. For crispier cookies use half the margarine and half the buttered flavored shortening called for in the recipe. Do not use baking powder and use a little less flour than your recipe requires.

8. How can I make great gravy for my roast chicken?

Chef Stefania: Try this idea. As an alternative to placing your chicken on a rack, prepare thick slices of onion and put them on a baking sheet. Next, place the chicken on top of the onions and bake the chicken so that the onions absorb the chicken juices. After the chicken is cooked, make your gravy by liquidizing the onion slices with chicken stock and white wine. Simmer the mixture for a few minutes and thicken it slightly with cornstarch.

9. Chef, I am confused about serving quantities when I boil rice and pasta. Help!

Chef Stefania: Here is a short list that may help you:

- 1 cup of uncooked rice makes 3 cups of cooked rice.
- 1 cup of cooked rice serves 2-3 people.
- 1 cup of dried macaroni makes 2½ cups of cooked macaroni.
- 1 cup of cooked macaroni serves 2 people.
- 8 ounces of packaged spaghetti makes 4 cooked cups and serves about 4 people.

For a more complete list, see the Measurement Conversion Charts link in the online Ultimate Food Scout (page 214).

10. My 4 kids love spaghetti. When I cook spaghetti sauce, I usually have some left over. Is there an easy way to keep this sauce and later use it for a quick impromptu meal?

    Chef Stefania: One idea is to freeze the sauce in ice cube trays. Once they're frozen, you can transfer the cubes to a sealable plastic freezer bag. Later you can reheat as many cubes as needed for a quick sauce for your kids. Also, I do the same thing when I have extra fresh lemon or lime juice. Later the juice can be thawed and used on food or to make a refreshing drink.

11. Chef, what's an easy way to cut vegetables into cubes?

    Chef Stefania: An easy way to cube vegetables is to use a product like Vidalia Chop Wizard. They can be purchased inexpensively from local retailers or online.

12. I've noticed that when serving my guests a dish with garlic, some later complain about gas. Is there a way to prepare garlic to minimize gas discomfort?

    Chef Stefania: Yes. You have to remove the garlic's core. Slice each clove length-wise. Use a knife to remove the core. Discard the core.

13. What hints can you give me on the best way to shop in a farmer's market?

    Chef Stefania: Your job is to select the freshest ingredients so use your sense of smell, touch, and sight. First, the products must look good. Next, smell items like melons and peaches. The best ones smell heavenly.

Organizational Skills

1. I was at a private dinner party in the Hamptons. You prepared an excellent meal for twelve demanding people where you alone were able to cook and serve. How were you able to do this?

    Chef Stefania: If you're cooking for someone, try to find out what they want early so you can create a planning and shopping list. Remember Caesar said, "Divide and conquer," so break your task list into unique small jobs. You will notice that even a small meal has many tasks, each of which takes time. Make sure your task list is in chronological order to make it easy for you to complete as many jobs as possible ahead of time.

2. I'm looking for a good program to help organize my recipes. Do you use one, and if so, which is the best?

    Chef Stefania: One of the top recipe organizer software packages is Cook'n. It has been reviewed on the Web, and you can easily purchase it from a variety of online sources.

Cook'n features include, for example, the ability to easily import recipes from the Web. Their interface aggregates recipes from a variety of websites, or you can easily input your own recipes. Also, the software provides the nutritional values for each recipe ingredient provided you use ingredients found in their food database. Plus, you can scale recipes if you need a different yield.

After you have input recipes, you can generate your own cookbook and sync your recipes to your various mobile devices. In addition, you can make a shopping list that estimates your bill making your meal preparation efficient and cost-effective.

Careers

1. I'm currently a cook working for a chain restaurant but have dreamed about being a private chef. What's the best way to get started?

Chef Stefania: To find a great job requires effort and luck. You can try the online sites but my experience is that networking works best.

This means you must be prepared and presentable. Work on a 30 second "Elevator" speech/pitch in which you emphasize what you can do for your employer. In most cases having a pleasing personality is just as important as being a great chef.

When working, you must be humble. Keep your hands moving. Be positive and listen well. Show that you love being a professional chef even if the environment is hot and the hours are long. Most important, be enthusiastic.

Also, try to find a job where you will be noticed such as a chef at a vacation villa or on a cruise ship. In these places you will have a chance to network. Try to meet people such as an "event planner." They have enormous knowledge of people who need private / personal chefs.

In addition, you can inexpensively make great double-sided business cards and personalized pens or magnets at websites such as Staples.com or Vistaprint.com. These make you look professional and help prospective customers remember you.

2. I'm considering a career as a chef. Is there a way that I can be tested so I'm assured that this is a good career choice before spending money on an expensive culinary school?

Chef Stefania: First, you must have a passion for cooking. Second, you must be able to easily work with people. Listening skills are important as is humility.

You can be assessed online from sites such as www.ggcareerservices.com. Also, if you are willing to take a community college class, there are counselors who can assist in developing a career life plan.

About Chef Stef

Have Spatula – Will Travel

Syros, the first port of Greece, is the capital of the Cycladic Islands. A four-hour boat trip from Athens will take you to this "mecca of culture." On this small island in the Aegean Sea a future chef was born several decades ago into a household with a very special vibrant room.

They say the kitchen is the heart of the home. It is where nutritious meals are crafted, where guests often socialize, and where countless hours of helping mom prepare holiday dinners have transpired.

We have memories of our mothers working tirelessly over crowded countertops and glowing stoves, preparing delectable, filling and wholesome meals that the family savored together.

Thus, a young Stefania became a culinary student learning the craft of cooking, and the joy of preparing family meals. It is a rite of passage when a child is entrusted family recipes to be enjoyed for years to come. As Stefania grew older, her palate hungered for the diverse wonders of food from other cultures.

Chef Stefania's culinary odyssey began taking her throughout Europe and from coast to coast in the United States living up to her motto, "Have Spatula – Will Travel." As a personal chef, this exciting journey provided her the opportunity to prepare cuisine for clients in locations such as Syros, Greece; Palm Beach, Florida; Bridgehampton, New York; Rancho Santa Fe and Laguna Beach, California. Her clients and their guests have included some of the most renowned and particular entrepreneurs, executives, politicians, entertainers, sports personalities and even an Academy Award-winning screenwriter.

While in Greece, Stefania was the owner of two restaurants where patrons enthusiastically consumed dishes made from her family's recipes enhanced with her special touch and personal recipes infused with world flavors. Patrons often commented, "You taught us how to eat."

As each restaurant rose in popularity, newspapers and magazines gave Stefania praise and recognition. This admiration resulted in Stefania becoming a guest chef on Greek television shows. Later, she was selected to be a member of the Greek Culinary Presentation Team for the "Flavors of the World Conference" held at the Culinary Institute of America in Napa, California.

An entrepreneurial client who has employed Stefania for the last nine years, and is responsible for the success of a major book distribution chain, urged Stefania to write a cookbook. His dinner guests thoroughly enjoyed her cuisine, and wanted to know when they could purchase Stefania's cookbook. Their comments and requests triggered the genesis of "Greek Cooking My Way."

This enthusiasm launched Stefania's cookbook creation pilgrimage. She assembled numerous traditional family recipes handed down to her through generations. Next, Stefania fused her own Greek recipes with world flavors she discovered on her frequent trips throughout the Mediterranean, Europe, South America, and the United States. The result is a clear step-by-step recipe roadmap with tips to enable the reader to perfectly recreate her cuisine.

Stefania's clients have bestowed on her phrases like: "You make us happy", "We love you", "Cook for us for life" and "You're a member of our family."

Stefania hopes that you will also enjoy her creations, the food that has delighted her family for generations.

"Stin eyasu"

("To Your Good Health")

Greek Cooking My Way Glossary

Cardamom Seeds

Cardamom is a pod consisting of an outer shell that has little flavor and with tiny inner seeds that have intense flavor. The cardamom seed has a complex flavor that can be described as slightly sweet and spicy with citric elements. It's a savory spice for curries, fish, meats, stews, poached dishes and sweet potatoes.

Coriander

The seeds are used as a spice. They are round-to-oval in shape, yellowish-brown in color with vertical ridges and have a flavor that is aromatic, sweet and citrusy, but also slightly peppery.

Coriander leaves, also known as cilantro, are a popular Mediterranean herb and often used in savory dishes in most parts of the world. The herb contains many notable plant derived chemical compounds that are known to have disease-preventing and health-promoting properties since it is very low in calories and contains no cholesterol. Its deep-green leaves possess good amounts of antioxidants, essential oils, vitamins, and dietary fiber, which help reduce LDL or "bad cholesterol" while raising HDL or "good cholesterol" levels. The seeds are also known for their anti-flatulent properties.

Cumin

A flowering plant that is native from the East Mediterranean to India. Its seeds are used in the cuisines of many different cultures in both whole and ground form. It is also used as a medicinal plant, serving as a digestant, as well as being used to treat anemia and the common cold.

Deglaze

Deglaze means to pour some cold liquid into a very hot frying or roasting pan to loosen up all the brown bits stuck to the bottom of the pan to make a very flavorful sauce. Those morsels, "fond," are where some of best the tastes are.

Feta Cheese

This cheese is a brined curd white cheese made in Greece from sheep's milk. Sometimes it's also made from a mixture of sheep's and goat's milk.

High quality feta should have a creamy texture. In the mouth it's tangy, slightly salty and mildly sour with a bit of a spicy finish, as well as a hint of sweetness.

It is used in many Greek dishes and salads. It tastes delicious with olive oil, oregano and roasted red peppers.

Filo Pastry

This pastry dough consists of paper thin sheets of unleavened flour dough separated by a thin film of butter. Filo can be used in many ways: layered, folded, rolled or ruffled with various fillings that are sweet or savory.

Commercially packaged frozen filo works well. When you use this filo, make sure it's defrosted properly and kept covered with a wet cloth napkin because it will dry quickly when it is exposed to air. Never handle filo with wet hands because it might tear.

Mastika Liqueur

Mastika (or Mastiha) comes from a tree called Skinos. Small cuts are made in the tree bark, which release tiny amounts of resin that are collected over 10 to 20 days during the months of June and July. This liqueur is produced on a Greek island called Chios.

It's excellent in an ice-cold shot glass as an aperitif or after dinner drink. It's also a good drink for digestion.

Mavrodafni Sweet Red Wine

This Greek wine is a dark, almost opaque liquid with a dark purple reflective color. It presents the aromas and flavors of caramel, chocolate, coffee, raisins and plums. It's similar to port wine.

You can use it for poaching fruit or making sauce. The sauce is excellent over pork or duck. Also, it can be consumed as a great dessert wine.

Mezze

A mezze is a collection of small dishes similar to appetizers served to accompany and complement drinks such as wine, ouzo, or tsipouro. The collection provides an excellent backdrop for social gatherings and enhances the dining experience.

Ouzo

This is a clear anise-flavored aperitif that is widely consumed in Greece and Cyprus. However, when water or ice is added, ouzo turns to a milky white color.

There is an old Greek saying that "ouzo makes the spirit." That's true since the Greek spirit is found in hearty food, soulful music and the love of lively conversation. A glass of chilled ouzo is a perfect companion to all these things.

Quince

Quince is a hard yellow fruit similar to a stocky green pear which usually cannot be eaten raw. They're very tart. But the tannins that cause the tartness in the raw fruit transform the quince, when cooked, into a tasty dish.

You can use them just like apples or pears. Compared to other fruits, quinces are relative high in pectin so jams and jellies made from this fruit will thicken and set.

Tasty quince preparation can be accomplished by a variety of other ways. They can be poached, preserved or added to apple pie as well as savory dishes such as stew or vegetables.

You can find quince from October to December in large supermarkets, farmers' markets or ethnic stores. Quinces also make a good table center piece and fill the entire room with their enticing scent.

Reserve

These are ingredients, mixtures, or preparations set aside for later use in cooking.

Rolling Boil

A condition of continuous rapid boiling that does not stop or slow when stirred. It is sometime referred to as a full rolling boil.

Saffron

Saffron is a spice derived from the flower crocus. The dried stigmas (thread-like parts of the flower) are used to make saffron spice.

Saffron is cultivated and harvested by hand. This makes saffron the most expensive spice by weight but a small amount is all that is needed. Consequently, a single gram of saffron easily transforms a dish into golden color with a fragrant scent.

Star Anise

This fruit originates from a tree in the magnolia family and enhances the flavor of meats, poultry, fish and fruit. Its strong flavor is sweet and licoricey. Also, use this beautiful star when concerned about your meal's visual appeal.

Tahini

This paste originates from ground sesame seeds. In Greece, tahini is used as a spread either alone or topped with honey or jam. Also, tahini can be mixed into soups, dressings, sauces or hummus. In addition, it can be made into sweet treats.

To Proof

In baking, the verb "to proof" refers to a test that describes the action to make certain dry yeast is still alive and ready to use in baking. The yeast is dissolved in warm sugar water before incorporating it into dough. After 5 or 10 minutes, the yeast should begin to form creamy foam on the water's surface. If this happens, the yeast is alive and you can proceed to combine the yeast mixture with the flour and other dry ingredients.

Tsipouro

The first production of Tsipouro was the work of Greek monks during the fourteenth century on Mount Athos in Macedonia, Greece. It's a strong distilled spirit containing 40-45 percent alcohol by volume. It is produced from the residue of the wine press and comes in two types, pure or anise flavor.

It is usually served in shot glasses with ice often with delicious mezze like feta, olives and nuts while having fun with friends, singing and dancing.

Turmeric

This is a popular spice in many Asian, Indian and Greek dishes. It also has a long history of medicinal uses with numerous studies validating its healing properties.

The active ingredient in turmeric is curcumin, which is known as a powerful antioxidant. It targets dangerous free radicals in the body reducing the damage they are able to cause DNA and cells. In addition, curcumin has anti-inflammatory qualities making it effective for fighting osteoarthritis pain and other health problems related to inflammation and heart disease.

It reduces the risk of blood clots and prevents the buildup of plaque in the arteries. This assists in the battle against stroke and other clot-related problems. Also, studies have shown turmeric is beneficial for reducing bad cholesterol and improving good cholesterol.

The Book Buyer's Bonus

www.chefsteflux.com/book

For my valued customers, I've created a "Bonus" page on my website. Follow these simple steps to access the supplementary content:

1. Enter https://chefsteflux.com/book in your browser.
2. Click on "Access Bonus Content."
3. Enter the password: bbb2017.

You'll find these extra resources:

The Ultimate Food Scout

See the following page for an explanation of these useful culinary links.

The Culinary Search Phrase Fest

A collection of helpful search phrases and search engines that will help you make great culinary searches.

Meta Search Engines for Recipes

A collection of recipe search engines that search multiple recipe sites simultaneously to help you find additional great recipes quickly!

- Bing Recipe Search
- Foodpair – Over 4.5 million recipes
- Recipe Bridge
- Tasty Query
- Yummly

Stefania's Specialty Menu Magazine

This magazine includes menus created from book recipes to help you plan for an exciting event. Included in the Menu Magazine are these innovative menus:

- The Easter Feaster
- Sexy Syros Brunch Munch
- The Mediterranean Spring Fling
- The Greek Christmas Dinner
- Romantic Athenian Dinner

The Ultimate Search Scout

- A collection of live search sites

The Ultimate Food Scout

A Collection of Useful Websites

The Ultimate Food Scout is a compilation of over 400 categorized, useful culinary Web links!

Some of the categories are: Culinary Dictionaries/Thesauri, Food/Ingredient Substitution, Meal Planning, Measurement Conversion Charts, Pick Your Own Fruits and Veggies, and Recipe Sites.

Visiting these culinary sites can help improve your cooking skills. I hope you visit the "The Ultimate Food Scout" and enjoy the available resources.

To visit this page:

1. Enter https://chefsteflux.com/book in your browser.
2. Click on "Access Bonus Content."
3. Enter the password: bbb2017.
4. Click on "The Ultimate Food Scout."

The Culinary Search Phrase Fest

This collection of helpful search phrases and search engines will help you make great culinary Web searches.

This tool provides you with advanced techniques to narrow your search in conjunction with 9 search engines to find what you want more easily.

To visit this page:

1. Enter https://chefsteflux.com/book in your browser.
2. Click on "Access Bonus Content."
3. Enter the password: bbb2017.
4. Click: "The Culinary Search Phrase Fest."

Index

D

E

F

G

H

I

N

O

P

Q

R

S

T

My Notes...

My Notes...

My Notes...

Contact Information

Let's Stay in Touch

I appreciate very much that you purchased **Greek Cooking My Way.** I hope you enjoy it. Your satisfaction is very important to me. All constructive comments are very welcome.

For additional information, please visit my website at: www.chefsteflux.com. In addition, if you forward me your E-mail, I will send you information about my future publications and events.

- E-mail stef@chefsteflux.com

You can also visit my social sites at:

- Facebook www.facebook.com/chefsteflux
- Twitter www.twitter.com/chefsteflux
- Instagram www.instagram.com/chefsteflux

I am very grateful for those who follow me on social media sites and am extremely thankful for those who "Like" my creations on those sites.

I look forward to staying in touch.

ΕΡΜΟΥ ΔΗΜΟΣ ΤΑΔ ΕΙΣΑΤΟ ΔΗΜΑΡΧΟΥΝΤΟΣ Δ ΒΑΦΙΑΔΑΚΗ

www.ingramcontent.com/pod-product-compliance
Lightning Source LLC
Chambersburg PA
CBHW040300100426
42811CB00011B/1320

9780999594902